Bible Bites

Daily Inspiration for the Soul

Dr. Shirley V. Clarke

Copyright © 2020 Dr. Shirley V. Clarke.

All rights reserved. No part of this book may be used or reproduced by any means, graphic, electronic, or mechanical, including photocopying, recording, taping or by any information storage retrieval system without the written permission of the author except in the case of brief quotations embodied in critical articles and reviews.

This book is a work of non-fiction. Unless otherwise noted, the author and the publisher make no explicit guarantees as to the accuracy of the information contained in this book and in some cases, names of people and places have been altered to protect their privacy.

WestBow Press books may be ordered through booksellers or by contacting:

WestBow Press
A Division of Thomas Nelson & Zondervan
1663 Liberty Drive
Bloomington, IN 47403
www.westbowpress.com
1 (866) 928-1240

Because of the dynamic nature of the Internet, any web addresses or links contained in this book may have changed since publication and may no longer be valid. The views expressed in this work are solely those of the author and do not necessarily reflect the views of the publisher, and the publisher hereby disclaims any responsibility for them.

Any people depicted in stock imagery provided by Getty Images are models, and such images are being used for illustrative purposes only. Certain stock imagery © Getty Images.

Interior Image Credit: Rinaldi Ledain

Scripture taken from the King James Version of the Bible.

Scripture taken from the Holy Bible: International Standard Version®. Copyright © 1996-forever by The ISV Foundation. ALL RIGHTS RESERVED INTERNATIONALLY. Used by permission.

THE HOLY BIBLE, NEW INTERNATIONAL VERSION®, NIV® Copyright © 1973, 1978, 1984, 2011 by Biblica, Inc.® Used by permission. All rights reserved worldwide.

Scripture taken from the Amplified Bible, Copyright © 1954, 1958, 1962, 1964, 1965, 1987 by The Lockman Foundation. Used with permission.

"Scripture quotations are from the ESV® Bible (The Holy Bible, English Standard Version®), copyright © 2001 by Crossway, a publishing ministry of Good News Publishers. Used by permission. All rights reserved."

ISBN: 978-1-9736-8012-3 (sc)
ISBN: 978-1-9736-8014-7 (hc)
ISBN: 978-1-9736-8013-0 (e)

Library of Congress Control Number: 2019919582

Print information available on the last page.

WestBow Press rev. date: 02/19/2020

Dedication

To the thousands of persons who have ever felt rejected or abandoned, those who have been hurt by those they trusted, those who have felt like giving up, and those who in spite of the trials and the struggles, still managed to make it one more day, one more mile.

And to Michaeljohn Clarke, for believing in my dream.

Acknowledgements

I would like to acknowledge my family who has been a support as this book grew. My siblings Gloria, Esther, David, and Victor who encouraged my journey. My mother Sherrel Rowe Boyce, who thought that my words were "so encouraging, others will be blessed by them also." My son Michaeljohn Clarke who told anyone who cared to listen, that his mother was "Truly the best, a teacher, preacher, encourager, and mother of the world, who has something to say, and something worth hearing." My job sister Julia Graham who consistently told me, "You are amazing. You are a motivation. You have something that the world needs." My church families for believing that the words were not just from my mind, but they were always a "Word from the Lord." I also acknowledge award winning author Nigeria Lockley who showed me that it could be done, even when your plate is already full. Finally, Jonathan Woods, for telling me that "If God didn't have a plan and purpose for you, He wouldn't have called you. So, do what He called you to do."

Thank you all.

Introduction

When I first started the work on this book, it was not supposed to be a book. It was a message that was sent to encourage someone who was dealing with the hardships of life. After I sent the message, I was invited to include others in "the next message." I prayed and asked God to send me a Word. I didn't want to share anything that was not according to the will or plan of God. Not only did I receive a Word, but I received a daily word for over three years. As one person read the messages, he or she would ask me to add a friend or relative to my daily message. Then, I noticed that I was being tagged on social media as others began posting the messages there. As "friends" read the messages on my page, I was invited to join other groups and asked to share my work. Then, I was asked, "When is the book coming out?"

I had not planned on writing a book, but it was suddenly a pressing question as readers became friends who had needs. Suddenly, it was not about the daily message, but it was about the lives that were being impacted by those messages. I had, at this time, been sharing the Word through my messages for four years, so I started compiling the posts. But was it enough to be a book? How would this work truly be impactful? I met with author Nigeria Lockley and discussed the birth of "Bible Bites." And so the dream became a vision. The vision became a reality.

As I look back over the years of writing, I clearly see that although I was writing as I received inspiration from God, I was also writing my story. The messages of hope, peace, forgiveness, love, and faith were the stories of my past fears and failures. I saw my hurt and pain, my shame and regret, all being exposed. But, I realize that I have been healing as I have been writing. The messages of forgiveness are the remnants of the pain I felt, but they are also a reflection of the joy I realized when I finally forgave and let go of my bitterness.

So, as this book becomes a reality, so too does my story become a reality. I have been hurt, rejected, abused, and despised. However, I have been loved, accepted, and forgiven, and that is the purpose of this book; to show the lost and abandoned that there is hope. There is love and forgiveness available to all who seek it. Trust me. I know. It just takes faith to make it real.

This year, be determined to be in charge of your failures and your successes. Let this be your year of letting go. Let go of presumptions and assumptions. Let go of jumping to conclusions and hasty decisions. Let go of narrow-mindedness and petty biases. Let go of dependency and reliance. Only by letting go of the things that control you can you be truly free to face your better self. Only by letting go of your need to control can you be free to let God be in control. And when God is in control, all will be better. Let go and Let God. And have a stress-free day.

> *Then he answered and spake unto me, saying, This is the word of the LORD unto Zerubbabel, saying, Not by might, nor by power, but by my spirit, saith the LORD of hosts. (Zechariah 4:6)*

> *And he said unto me, My grace is sufficient for thee: for my strength is made perfect in weakness. Most gladly therefore will I rather glory in my infirmities, that the power of Christ may rest upon me. (2 Corinthians 12:9)*

What are three things that you must let go of to be free to be your true self?

1. _____
2. _____
3. _____

What are three things that you can do to become your true self?

1. _____
2. _____
3. _____

Over the past year, there have been many persons you allowed into your inner space. You allowed them rights and privileges that should not have been given. Now, as you are about to leave the old year behind, take back what rightfully belongs to you. Take back the right to be happy, the right to be honest, the right to laugh when humor strikes, and the right to cry when sorrow comes. Take back the freedom that was afforded at the cross. You were given the right to be called the child of God, heir, and joint heir with Christ. Therefore, you have the privilege of being called royalty. That's a right you must reclaim as you begin the new life that Christ has prepared for you in the new year. Leave the old year with a new classification: free citizen, child of the King. And have a renewed day.

> *Therefore if any man be in Christ, he is a new creature: old things are passed away; behold, all things are become new. (2 Corinthians 5:17)*

What are the things that you have allowed to be stolen from you?

1. _____
2. _____
3. _____
4. _____

List one thing that you need to reclaim today.

1. _____

List two things which you need to reclaim this coming month.

1. _____
2. _____

When you woke up this morning, what did you think of first? Did you think of the awesome love of God, His goodness, and mercy? Did you think of how He brought you through the night, safe and restored? Did you think about the fact that you are yet alive? Did you think to stop and have a conversation with Him, even if only for a few minutes? If there be any virtue, and if there be any praise, think on these things. And have an inspirational day.

> *Finally, brethren, whatsoever things are true, whatsoever things are honest, whatsoever things are just, whatsoever things are pure, whatsoever things are lovely, whatsoever things are of good report; if there be any virtue, and if there be any praise, think on these things. (Philippians 4:8)*

What are you thankful for right now? Take five minutes to tell the Lord what you are thankful for. This could be anything, no matter how small.

_____
_____
_____
_____
_____
_____

What is purpose? Purpose is the reason you get up in the morning and get out of your comfort zone. It's the thing that motivates you to keep on going even when you think you can't go on. It's the idea that stirs your passion enough for you to do the same thing day after day, and still love doing it. Purpose comes from God and is given to help you find your place in this world. If you lack it, He invites you to ask of Him, and He promises that you shall find it in Him. Purpose keeps you alive, so ask. And have a motivated day.

> *And whatsoever ye shall ask in my name, that will I do, that the Father may be glorified in the Son. If ye shall ask any thing in my name, I will do it. (John 14: 13, 14)*

1. If you were living your true "purpose," what would your day look like?

   _____
   _____
   _____
   _____
   _____

2. What is one thing that you can accomplish today to get you closer to that purpose described above?

   _____
   _____
   _____
   _____
   _____
   _____

Perseverance seldom fails. But if it does, get right back on that horse and keep on riding. You can do all things through Christ who strengthens you. The good thing about riding a horse is that after a few minutes, the horse takes over, and you just have to move with the rhythm of the ride. So it is with getting the job done. If you stick with it, after a while, it becomes natural. So, don't give up. Keep riding, because the finish line is near, and the judge is waiting to reward your efforts. Keep pressing. And have a determined day.

I can do all things through Christ which strengtheneth me. (Philippians 4:13)

Think of something that you tried and failed at. List the things that went wrong.

1. _____
2. _____
3. _____
4. _____
5. _____
6. _____
7. _____
8. _____
9. _____
10. _____

What you would do differently if given the opportunity?

I would:

_____
_____
_____
_____
_____

Life is too precious to stay quiet while someone walks all over you. If you are being walked on, or over, you've already bent too low before that someone. The minute that you stand up and stand tall, he or she will lose his or her footing. No one can walk on you while your head is held high. Remember, they will eventually become your foot stool. So stand tall. And have a conqueror's day.

> *And David himself saith in the book of Psalms, The Lord said unto my LORD, Sit thou on my right hand. Till I make thine enemies thy footstool. (Luke 20: 42, 43)*
>
> *Write out a message to yourself detailing how you will handle a difficult but familiar situation today. What will you say or do to ensure that you will be victorious in the eyes of man and God?*

Dear self,

_____
_____
_____
_____
_____
_____
_____
_____
_____
_____

Many of you want healing, unconditionally. You want God to hear you, unconditionally. You want your sins forgiven, unconditionally. However, there are conditions to be met. If you just humble yourself, pray from a heart of thirst, and seek His face like one seeks for the rain in a time of drought, He will hear you, He will forgive you, and He will heal you. Those are the conditions to be met. So be prepared to receive only if you are willing to act. And have a restoration day.

> *If my people, who are called by my name, will humble themselves and pray and seek my face and turn from their wicked ways, then I will hear from heaven, and I will forgive their sin and will heal their land. (2 Chronicles 7:14)*

1. What do you earnestly desire from God for your spiritual growth?

   _____
   _____
   _____
   _____
   _____

2. What are you willing to commit to in order to achieve this goal?

   _____
   _____
   _____
   _____
   _____

It's amazing what praising will do. But it's simply awesome what worship will accomplish. Praise is the outward expression of inward worship. Praise exalts the Lord, while worship exalts the relationship. If you've only been praising but not worshipping, now is the time to shift the relationship. Now is the time to gain access to His secret place. Now is the time to move from servant to friend. From friend to child. It doesn't mean that you stop praising. It just means that you worship Him with your level of praise. Worship Him today in the Spirit. And have a spiritually elevated day.

> *Give unto the LORD the glory due unto his name; worship the LORD in the beauty of holiness. (Psalms 29:2)*

> *But the hour cometh, and now is, when the true worshippers shall worship the Father in spirit and in truth: for the Father seeketh such to worship him. God is a Spirit: and they that worship him must worship him in spirit and in truth. (John 4:23, 24)*

How will you express and elevate your level of worship today? List three things that you will express to God to show your appreciation.

1. _____
2. _____
3. _____

List three things that you will do differently in your praise.

1. _____
2. _____
3. _____

Be thankful for what you have and for what God did not allow you to get. Be thankful for those who are in your life and on your side, and for those who left you, because they would have messed you up if they had stayed. Be thankful for the job and paycheck, and for the fact that your credit score isn't where it should be right now, so that you cannot get another card to max out for those special occasions. But most of all, be thankful for *life*, *love*, and *liberty*, because they really are all that you have, and in this day and age they can be taken or lost in the blink of an eye. So be thankful. And have an appreciative day.

> *In every thing give thanks: for this is the will of God in Christ Jesus concerning you. (1 Thessalonians 5:18)*

What are at least four things which you "lost" or were taken away from you over the past years that you can finally appreciate not having in your life?

1. _____
2. _____
3. _____
4. _____

What are the positive results to not having these individual "burdens" to carry?

1. _____
2. _____
3. _____
4. _____

Offer a short prayer of thanks for your deliverance.

The fact that at some point in your life you will need to wear spectacles is important. Sometimes you will be able to see things clearly, and sometimes, you won't. That's why you are instructed not to judge others. Things are not always what you think they are, and clarity is often needed. Just as you go for your eye exam and accept the fact that your vision has changed, so it must be with your life. When things are no longer clear, ask for clarity to understand before you judge or jump to conclusions. Remember, if you judge others with your blurred understanding, you will also be judged. And Christ sees all, and clearly. So withhold judgment. And have a self-check day.

> *Judge not, that ye be not judged. For with what judgment ye judge, ye shall be judged: and with what measure ye mete, it shall be measured to you again. And why beholdest thou the mote that is in thy brother's eye, but considerest not the beam that is in thine own eye? (Matthew 7:1, 2, 3)*

What is something or someone that you have been judgmental about recently?

_____
_____
_____
_____

What are some similarities that you share with this person or situation?

_____
_____
_____
_____

Can you make the situation or person better with your judgment? How?

_____
_____
_____

Forgive yourself for your judgmental attitude and find something about the situation or person to appreciate.

Loving someone who is undeserving or who doesn't love you back can be heartbreaking. Love them anyway. Love is of God, love is divine, and love is a privilege. Don't love because you are loved. Love because when you were undeserving and wasn't even thinking about Him, Christ loved you. Love because you are a child of God, and He loves through you. Love because if you do not, you will hate, and hate destroys both body and soul. So as difficult as it may be, love, because, God loved you first. And have a reciprocal day.

> *Herein is love, not that we loved God, but that he loved us, and sent his Son to be the propitiation for our sins. Beloved, if God so loved us, we ought also to love one another. (1 John 4:10, 11)*

What are three things about you which make you loveable?

1. _____
2. _____
3. _____

What is something that makes you unlovable?

1. _____

How would others treat you if they knew this about you, and how would you feel?

Others would:
_____
_____
_____

I would feel:
_____
_____
_____
_____

Today, find someone you think is "unlovable" and show them love.

There are some vessels which you never use, except for special occasions. Then there are those which are used daily. It doesn't mean that they aren't all valuable. It simply means that every vessel has its time and purpose. You are a vessel, made with a purpose. Just because it seems like you aren't on the top shelf of someone's life, it doesn't mean that you aren't valuable to them. You serve a purpose that no one else can. Be patient. They will soon see their need of you. A vessel made for honor cannot be used as one made for dishonor. So be patient because your time is coming. And have an expectant day.

> *But in a great house there are not only vessels of gold and of silver, but also of wood and of earth; and some to honour, and some to dishonor. If a man therefore purge himself from these, he shall be a vessel unto honour, sanctified, and meet for the master's use, and prepared unto every good work. (2 Timothy 2: 20, 21)*

What qualifies you as an unfit vessel?
_____
_____
_____
_____

What do you need to do to in order to be "used" for service?
_____
_____
_____
_____

What qualifies you as a vessel of honor?
_____
_____
_____
_____

What are three things that you do daily to ensure that you are ready to be used?

1. _____
2. _____
3. _____

When the phone rings, do you rush to answer? Is it because you know who is on the other end? Were you anticipating the call, waiting impatiently to hear that voice on the line? Do you recognize the person who is calling before he or she says who it is? Is that how it is when the Master calls you? Are you anticipating his call, recognizing His voice immediately? Or does he have to reintroduce Himself each time He contacts you? When God has to try to get you to respond, to answer, to recognize His voice, there isn't anything wrong with the line. But, there is something very wrong with the relationship. It's time to fix what's broken, to get the connection working again. Be ready to answer when He calls. And have a responsive day.

> *My sheep hear my voice, and I know them, and they follow me: (John 10:27, 28)*

What are three things that you need to fix in your relationship with God?

1. _____
2. _____
3. _____

Begin working on fixing those issues, today.

Have you ever been in a fight? A real "I'm not walking away if you're walking away" fight. A fight where when it's over, you have to search for your shoes? Did you win? Was your opponent worthy? Do you think you did your best and handled it like a champion? Well, there's a battle you are facing every day, and the reason you aren't winning is because you think you're still fighting the same childhood fights, with the same equal opponents. But the scripture states that you wrestle not against flesh and blood, but against principalities and powers; against spiritual wickedness in high places. If you aren't equipped for battle, you won't only lose your shoes, you'll lose your life. So be armed, be prepared. And have a triumphant day.

> *For we wrestle not against flesh and blood, but against principalities, against powers, against the rulers of the darkness of this world, against spiritual wickedness in high places. (Ephesians 6:12)*

What was your last fight about?
_____
_____

Who won?
_____
_____

Was it worth it? Why or why not?
_____
_____

How would you fight differently next time?
_____
_____

List three things that you are tired fighting over.

1. _____
2. _____
3. _____

BIBLE BITES

Think of a first step toward resolving each of these issues.

1. _____
2. _____
3. _____

There are some mistakes that you make which cannot be corrected. These aren't the "apologize and move on" types. These are the "I can't believe I did that, said that, meant that" type. You go through life beating yourself up, and for what? The scripture states that if you confess your sins, He is faithful and just to forgive them. So stop holding yourself hostage to past mistakes, and take God at His word. He forgives you. Case closed. So accept the redemption that is freely given. And have a restored day.

> *If we confess our sins, he is faithful and just to forgive us our sins, and to cleanse us from all unrighteousness. (1 John 1:9)*

What is something that you are beating yourself up over? Why?

_____
_____
_____
_____

What are two strategies which you can implement to avoid repeating this "behavior"?

1. _____
_____
_____
_____
_____

2. _____
_____
_____
_____
_____

One problem with running a race is that you have others who are aiming for the same reward as you are. However, only one person gets the gold. But does that stop you from running? No, It doesn't. So why would you give up when life gets in the way of your spiritual race? When no matter how you place, your reward is sure? Where you are guaranteed gold, even if you get there after someone else fouled you out, or tripped you up? Don't forget, the race is not for the swift, but for those who endure to the end. Keep running. And have a rewarding day.

> *I returned, and saw under the sun, that the race is not to the swift, nor the battle to the strong, neither yet bread to the wise, nor yet riches to men of understanding, nor yet favour to men of skill; but time and chance happeneth to them all. (Ecclesiastes 9:11)*

Whom, or what, are you in competition with?

_____
_____
_____
_____

What are the obstacles to your winning?

1. _____
2. _____
3. _____
4. _____

What plan can you implement today that will improve your chances of winning?

_____
_____
_____
_____
_____
_____

Rejection does one of two things. It breaks you, or it makes you. If you allow it to define who you are, it will break your spirit and break your will. If you realize who you are, it will make you stronger, make you wiser, make you more of a reflection of God's peace. Remember, you are not how others treat you. You are not what others say that you are. You are a peculiar person, bought with the blood of Jesus. Instead of rejection, He chose you. So don't allow a "no" to be your compass. Your "Yes" is just ahead. So, accept His choosing. And have an affirmative day.

> *But you are a chosen people, a royal priesthood, a holy nation, God's special possession, that you may declare the praises of him who called you out of darkness into his wonderful light. (1 Peter 2:9) (NIV)*
>
> *What is one area of your life where you feel rejection or isolation? (Job, personal relationship, friendships, church?)*

_____

_____

_____

_____

How has this impacted you negatively and positively?

_____

_____

_____

_____

What has this shown you about your weaknesses or strengths?

_____

_____

_____

_____

How can you use this knowledge to take one step toward building your self-esteem?

Do you ever think you've figured it all out? You know what the situation is, how it got to this point, and exactly what will happen next? You already know what you will do when next happens? You've got the right words, facial expression, and body posture ready to go? Then God steps in and changes the situation so drastically, you are left wondering, "What did I miss"? Well God says He is the one who determines what happens next. He says it's not even a battle you are in. It's only a test. So stop preparing for a war when it's only a debate you are about to face. Your "next" is God's opportunity to prove that no weapon formed against you shall prosper. God's got this. So relax, and let the situation go. And have a victorious day.

> *Then Jesus answered and said unto her, O woman, great is thy faith: be it unto thee even as thou wilt. And her daughter was made whole from that very hour. (Matthew 15:28)*

> *For our light affliction, which is but for a moment, worketh for us a far more exceeding and eternal weight of glory; (2 Corinthians 4:17)*

What is something in your life that you are still trying to figure out? Why?

_____
_____
_____

What is something that you have all figured out?

_____
_____
_____
_____

What are two things that helped you with the latter accomplishment which you can apply to the former situation?

_____
_____
_____
_____

Challenge yourself today to do something great. Do more than you did yesterday. Go beyond the requirements of the task or your job. Ask someone how you can make their day better. Then do it if it's possible. All the stresses of yesterday will be erased if you just think of how you can make someone smile today. In short, show someone the love of God. Your world will be better for it. Give as you would want others to give to you. And have a charitable day.

> *Let nothing be done through strife or vainglory; but in lowliness of mind let each esteem other better than themselves. (Philippians 2:3)*

What is a goal that you will set for yourself for today?

_____
_____
_____
_____

How do you plan on realizing this goal?

_____
_____
_____
_____

How will it help others?

_____
_____
_____
_____

Life is like an automobile. You have it, you appreciate having it, but you have to maintain it. When anything goes wrong in it or with it, you immediately grow concerned and find someone or something to fix it. But there comes a time when that automobile has reached its last leg and you have to decide what to do with it. Don't let your life be the car that ends up in the junk yard. Live such a life of purpose that you will be repurposed for the good of others. In short, leave a legacy that others can follow. And have a productive day.

> *One generation shall praise thy works to another, and shall declare thy mighty acts. (Psalm 145:4)*
>
> *Train up a child in the way he should go: and when he is old, he will not depart from it. (Proverbs 22:6)*
>
> *And the things you have heard me say in the presence of many witnesses entrust to reliable people who will also be qualified to teach others. (2 Timothy 2:2) (AMPV)*

Commit to doing at least one thing today that will ensure that you leave a legacy for others to follow. What will that thing be? How will it help others?

Stop waiting until you get to school to learn. Stop waiting until you get a job to be productive. Stop waiting until you get to church to worship. Stop waiting until the children are grown to live. Stop waiting until it's too late to appreciate the things you had and the opportunities you missed. The scripture tells us that we must arise now while it is day, when it is time to work. The night is coming when you will not be able to do the things you could have done or should have done. And since you have to give an account for the talents you were given, why not have a good report to give? Live purposefully. And have an intentional day

> *I must work the works of him that sent me, while it is day: the night cometh, when no man can work. (John 9:4)*

> *So then every one of us shall give account of himself to God. (Romans 14:12)*

What are two things that you have been putting on hold?

1. _____

_____

2. _____

_____

What are the obstacles that are getting in the way?

1. _____

_____

2. _____

_____

Write a plan for overcoming one of these obstacles this week, then act on it.

_____

_____

_____

_____

Record the results of the plan that you acted on this week? If not fulfilled, what do you need to further do or work on to bring your plan to fulfillment?

_____
_____
_____
_____
_____

When the weather outside starts growing cold, you put away the warm-weather gear. You take out the sweaters, gloves, and boots. You cover the outside furniture. You check that the heating system is working, and all the radiators are clear. Yet when your spiritual climate starts to get chilly, you sit back and decide you don't need to bother because you know it will get better eventually. Really? Stop waiting for God to warm you up, and start putting away the things that are allowing you to stay spirituality cold. Plug in to the spiritual source and get on fire for God. Time is running out. Don't allow yourself to become spiritually frozen. Plug in. And have a recharged day.

> *Wherefore, seeing we also are compassed about with so great a cloud of witnesses, let us lay aside every weight, and the sin which doth so easily beset us, and let us run with patience the race that is set before us. (Hebrews 12:1)*

Determine which area of your spiritual relationship needs attention. Where are you "cold"?

___

___

___

What do you think is the cause of this?

___

___

___

___

Spend at least three minutes daily talking to God about your relationship and what you really want in it. Listen for the answer as you read the Word daily.

Record what you want in your spiritual relationship.

___

___

___

___

BIBLE BITES

List three things revealed from your daily study of the Word that need your attention to improve your relationship with God. Work on these things.

1. _____
2. _____
3. _____

When your heart feels heavy and tears are not far off, there are two choices. Just cry and let it all out, or don't cry and hold it all in. If you cry, you admit defeat, and if you don't, you appear indifferent. Just remember that even Jesus cried. And, it was all for the glory of God. So, if you cry, let it be godly sorrow, and if you don't, let it be divine temperance. Whatever you do, let God gain the glory. And have a comforted day

> *And whatsoever ye do in word or deed, do all in the name of the Lord Jesus, giving thanks to God and the Father by him. (Colossians 3:17)*

Describe the last situation that brought you to tears.

_____
_____
_____
_____

If you cannot remember the last time you cried, what, or who, is it that makes it difficult for you to give in to your emotions?

_____
_____
_____
_____

What would it look like to just let it all out? If I cried ...

_____
_____
_____
_____

What would happen if you were honest with yourself 100 percent? Would you find anything about you that wasn't good enough? Would you identify the actions and attitudes that require change? Would you look at your physical self and be happy with what you see, or admit that something needed fixing? Would you confess that some of your desires are of the things of this world, but clearly not of God? If you cannot be honest with yourself, how can you judge him or her? How can you tell them that they are wrong for what they said or did? That mote in your eye can be blinding, but the scripture says that "you" are the one who can remove it. Remember that freedom comes with the truth, so now is the time for honesty. Be real with yourself. And have a self-evaluating day

> *And why beholdest thou the mote that is in thy brother's eye, but considerest not the beam that is in thine own eye?" (Matthew 7:3)*

> *And ye shall know the truth, and the truth shall make you free. (John 8:32)*

What are two things about your behavior that you have not been truthful about? What can you do to change these behaviors?

1. _____

Change:
_____

2. _____

Change:
_____

What are two things about your physical self that you need to address? What can you do today to begin addressing these issues?

1. _____

Change:
_____

2. _____

Change:
_____

Have you ever been called out for something you've done? Maybe it was a parent who called your entire name. First, middle, and last. You knew you were in big trouble then. You started thinking of all the excuses you would make to avoid punishment, but of course, nothing helped. What about school? The principal calls your name over the intercom, and you and the whole school froze, just because you knew? What will your reaction be when your name is called before Christ? Will you think of excuses? Or will you just freeze in fear? That time may soon be here, so get your act together, so that you need not fear or look for excuses. God's punishment is greater than parent or principal. So, live blameless. And have a guilt free day.

> *For we must all appear before the judgment seat of Christ; that every one may receive the things done in his body, according to that he hath done, whether it be good or bad. (2 Corinthians 5:10)*

What would God "call you out" for, if you stood before Him right now?

_____
_____
_____
_____

What excuse do you have to give God about the thing He has "called you out for"?

_____
_____
_____
_____

Write a short prayer asking God to forgive you. Commit to avoiding falling into the same situation again.

_____
_____
_____
_____

Have you ever just stopped to watch a carpenter at work? Did you consider the way he measured, leveled, marked, and cut? The way attention was given to the smallest detail? That's because if it's a house that's being built, someone has to live in it. It has to be able to handle the wear and tear of daily living. It must withstand all weather changes. It must protect its family from harm and danger. That's why you were created by the Master carpenter. Your house is his abode. You were created to withstand all outside attacks. After all of the attention that went into crafting you, you'd think you'd take good care of His temple. Remember you were built to house a king. Treat his masterpiece as the jewel that it is. And have a sanctified day.

> *Know ye not that your bodies are the members of Christ? shall I then take the members of Christ, and make them the members of an harlot? God forbid. What? know ye not that your body is the temple of the Holy Ghost which is in you, which ye have of God, and ye are not your own? For ye are bought with a price: therefore glorify God in your body, and in your spirit, which are God's. (1 Corinthians 6:15, 19, 20)*

What are you doing to maintain the house that you live in, spiritually, and naturally?

_____
_____
_____
_____

What are the little details that you need to attend to before a problem develops?

1. _____
2. _____
3. _____
4. _____
5. _____

Begin today to repair what's already broken.

Whatever your challenge is today, pray. When voices rise up against you, pray. When the enemy comes in like a flood, pray. When the friend you trusted to have your back becomes a colleague who wants your spot, pray. Today you will need all the resources of heaven to get out of that corner you have been backed into. Just pray. The test you were under is about to be over. Just watch God answer. He will. Just believe. And have a winning day.

> *Be careful for nothing; but in every thing by prayer and supplication with thanksgiving let your requests be made known unto God. (Philippians 4:6)*
>
> *Pray without ceasing. (1 Thessalonians 5:17)*

List five things that you need to pray about today.

1. _____
2. _____
3. _____
4. _____
5. _____

Decide which one you believe is the most important and go into a season of praying and fasting just for that one.

After a week, record the outcome of your prayers. Then, do the same for the second. Repeat for all thing from your list.

Week 1.
_____
_____

Week 2.
_____
_____

Week 3.
_____
_____

Week 4.
_____
_____

Week 5.
_____
_____

Have you ever felt like the more you try to walk uprightly, the harder and more unstable the road becomes? The more you try to climb those mountains, the steeper the way becomes? There is nothing wrong with the path or the mountains. It's all up to you to change in order to handle the obstacles. So if the way is rough or the mountain too steep, check your shoes. If you are not prepared for the rough journey, you won't get far on the climb. Check your shoes. Preparation is always necessary before you start a task. And the wrong gear will slow you down or stop your progress. So let your feet be shod with the preparation of the gospel of peace. Check your shoes. And have a secure day.

> *Stand therefore, having your loins girt about with truth, and having on the breastplate of righteousness; And your feet shod with the preparation of the gospel of peace; (Ephesians 6:14, 15)*

What is one area of your life that is requiring you to change?
_____
_____
_____

Are you resistant? Why?
_____
_____
_____

What would change look like?
_____
_____
_____

Commit to one small change today. Record the results of that change.
_____
_____
_____

Repeat as needed.

As convenient as technology has become, there are still flaws. Things can overload, slow down, or crash. There are documents that are mysteriously deleted, and folders where things can be hidden from the eyes of others. So it is with our lives. There are things that overload your brains, slow them down, and that we totally lose from our memories. Then there are things that we choose to keep from others, hoping that these things will never be found. But God uses His omnipotence to keep record of your every thought, word, and deed. With Him, you can't hide the truth, so it's better to keep your life well organized, backed up by the Holy Spirit, and your inner drive clean. It's the only way to keep your spirit running well. Declutter. And have a consecrated day.

> *Thou knowest my downsitting and mine uprising, thou understandest my thought afar off. (Psalm 139:2)*

If you had to declutter your mind or delete some things from your thoughts, what are four things that you would delete?

1. _____
2. _____
3. _____
4. _____

What are four things that you would upload to replace the deleted "files" of your mind?

1. _____
2. _____
3. _____
4. _____

Do It.

After the storm is ended, after the thunder has quieted, after the lightening has stopped its flashing, and after the waters have subsided, you will still be standing. You may be wet, shivering, and even sneezing a bit, but you will be standing. You have the assurance that in the midst of every storm, there is Christ. And at the end of the rainstorm, there is a rainbow. But at the source of the winds, there is God. He is in control. So when it is all over, be confident of this one thing, you will be standing. Fear not. And have a grounded day.

> *Wherefore take unto you the whole armour of God, that ye may be able to withstand in the evil day, and having done all, to stand. Stand therefore, having your loins girt about with truth, and having on the breastplate of righteousness;*
> *(Ephesians 6:13, 14)*

Describe a situation where your faith has been tested this past week?

_____
_____
_____
_____

Were you able to stand on your faith? Why or why not?

_____
_____
_____
_____
_____

What encouraging words would you tell someone who is going to face the situation you did?

_____
_____
_____
_____
_____

One day you will wake up and realize that all the sacrifices you made were for persons with their own agenda. You will find that "I love you" meant "I needed you for a time or season." You will understand that "I will never leave you", meant "until times get too hard or the situation too difficult." But there is a sacrifice that was made for you, and a promise that was given. God will never leave you nor forsake you, no matter how difficult things may become. He really does love you; with an everlasting love. So don't sweat the things you can't control. He is for real. Accept His love. And have a treasured day.

> *When my father and my mother forsake me, then the LORD will take me up. (Psalm 27:10)*
>
> *The LORD hath appeared of old unto me, saying, Yea, I have loved thee with an everlasting love: therefore with lovingkindness have I drawn thee. (Jeremiah 31:3)*

What were the promises made to you that were never kept?

_____
_____
_____
_____

What made it harder to accept? The promises that you were hoping would be kept or the person who disappointed you?

_____
_____
_____
_____

What are some promises which God has made to you that He has kept?

_____
_____
_____
_____

Forgive the ones who failed you. Rest in the fact that God will always keep His promises.

If you are using daily moisturizer to help you stay young, or look young, think again. Does that stuff do what it's expected to? Does it turn back the years, and help you regain the prime of your life? Then let me remind you of something that not only turns back the hands of time, but helps you live eternally. It's the blood of Jesus. And unlike these miracle cures, it will cost you absolutely nothing, just faith. Just think, no Botox, no surgery, nothing but the blood of Jesus. He will beautify you with His salvation. So trust Him, and try him. And have a transforming day.

> *For the LORD taketh pleasure in his people: he will beautify the meek with salvation. (Psalm 149:4)*

Try one of these things if you want to stay young longer:

1. Throw a coin in a fountain and make a wish.
2. Draw, color, or doodle for 30 minutes.
3. Go to a drive-in movie.
4. Write your spouse a love letter.

Try one of these things if you want to live eternally:

1. Show gratitude every day.
2. Love others as you love yourself.
3. Treat others the way you want to be treated.
4. Trust in the Lord with all your heart.
5. Believe on the Lord Jesus Christ.

Check off when completed.

When you hear a car alarm sounding, what do you imagine? Someone is attempting to break in? Or maybe someone got too close to the sensor? What about a house alarm? Do you imagine seeing the cops coming, someone being taken away? What about your morning alarm? Do you still look to see if it's really the alarm, or really the time it's supposed to be? When Christ sounds the alarm for His coming, you won't have time to think, imagine, or check that things are as they should be. Living in a state of unpreparedness can cost you here and before the Lord. For at such an hour as you think not, the Son of Man shall appear. The alarm is already set, and you don't know when it will sound, so be ready and stay ready. And have a prepared day.

> *Therefore be ye also ready: for in such an hour as ye think not the Son of man cometh. (Mathew 24:44)*

What do you still need to do to be sure you are ready if Christ should appear today?

_____
_____
_____
_____

What do you believe in? Are you focused on family, the love of your life, your job, possessions, or something else? What makes you the happiest? That's the thing you can't do without. That's what you believe in. But, remember that God has said that if you believe in Him, you shall have everlasting life. That is the only person or thing that can bring true happiness. He also said that He is a jealous God. So, be careful not to replace the Creator with the created. And put not your confidence in man. Man will fail, but God never will. So today, believe in God. And have a hallowed day.

> *He that believeth on the Son hath everlasting life: and he that believeth not the Son shall not see life, but the wrath of God abides upon him. (John 3:36)*
>
> *For thou shalt worship no other god: for the LORD, whose name is Jealous, is a jealous God: (Exodus 34:12)*

Who are two persons that you believe you cannot do without?

1. _____
2. _____

What is something that they contribute to your living?

_____
_____
_____
_____

What is something that they cannot do for you, even if they wanted to?

_____
_____
_____
_____

Ask God to fill the place that man cannot fill. Then, offer a prayer of appreciation for all that He has done and is doing in your life.

Strength and power are in the tongue. Speak your victory and deliverance into existence. Declare that it is done. Claim that the battle is over, then, plan your celebration. It's no use living by faith when works are absent. And it's pointless to attempt the impossible when faith is weak. So step out on the promises of God and recognize the power in your words. If you ask anything, according to His will, it shall be accomplished. So claim your inheritance today. Be delivered. And have a conqueror's day

> *Death and life are in the power of the tongue: and they that love it shall eat the fruit thereof. (Proverbs 18:21)*
>
> *For as the body without the spirit is dead, so faith without works is dead also. (James 2:26)*
>
> *And whatsoever ye shall ask in my name, that will I do, that the Father may be glorified in the Son. If ye shall ask any thing in my name, I will do it. (John 14:13, 14)*

Create a list of at least ten affirmations that you will repeat each day when you get out of bed and before you go to bed each night. Use the promises that God has made to you as a starting point for your affirmations.

One example could be, "I am the head and not the tail."

1. _____
2. _____
3. _____
4. _____
5. _____
6. _____
7. _____
8. _____
9. _____
10. _____

Why is it that you feel challenged to show the world who you are? You are your own woman or man? You are an adult and can do what you want to? You are old enough to make your own decisions? You need to prove to somebody that you have it together, and you are over them? Stop proving to others what you are and prove to God who you are supposed to be. You are bought with a price. Therefore, you are not your own. The only one whose opinion matters is Christ. Stop proving and start proofing. The life you live for Christ is the only proof the world needs. That will be enough. Honor Him with your living. And have a purified day.

> *What? know ye not that your body is the temple of the Holy Ghost which is in you, which ye have of God, and ye are not your own? (1 Corinthians 6:19)*

What are three things that you do to please others?

1. _____
   _____
2. _____
   _____
3. _____
   _____

How do these things conflict with who God says you are and/or what He expects of you?

_____
_____
_____
_____

Who do you really want to please? God or man? Begin today to align your life with what God says about you and with what He expects from you.

Whatever it takes, be the peacemaker in your own battle. Don't wait for something miraculous to happen. There isn't going to be a knock on the door and a visitor waiting to give you an answer from heaven. There isn't going to be a phone call to soothe the anger and hurt you are feeling. There is only the word of God that lives in you. His peace He leaves with you, so that you may always be at peace. So be the peacemaker in your own struggle. Remember it begins inside. So seek peace and pursue it. And have a calm day.

> *Peace I leave with you, my peace I give unto you: not as the world giveth, give I unto you. Let not your heart be troubled, neither let it be afraid. (John 14:27)*

What is something that you have been struggling with that has taken your peace away?

_____
_____
_____
_____

What steps can you take to regain that peace?

_____
_____
_____
_____

Decide what you need to let go of or what you need to begin doing to regain your peace.

List three things that you will let go of and three things that you will begin to do in order to attain that peace that you so desire.

I will release:

1. _____
2. _____
3. _____

I will commit to doing:

1. _____
2. _____
3. _____

Remember, you are in control of how you respond to the triggers around you. Choose peace.

Today, when you get the chance to speak out against some injustice, don't walk away. Speak out. When you see the opportunity to stand up and help some person who cannot be heard, remember what Christ said. "As much as you do it unto one of these, you do it unto Me." If you turn your back on the defenseless, you turn your back on Him. So stand and represent Christ, and He will stand up for you when you need Him most. Speak out. And have a commendable day

> *And the King shall answer and say unto them, Verily I say unto you, Inasmuch as ye have done it unto one of the least of these my brethren, ye have done it unto me." (Matthew 25:40)*

What cause can you champion today?
_____
_____
_____
_____

Who can you speak up for today?
_____
_____
_____
_____

If you don't already have a cause, find something or someone to speak out about or for today.

When you get tired of asking someone to do what they promised, you often remind them of the many times you asked, and waited, and yet you are still waiting. But, when you think of the goodness of Jesus, and all He has done for you, do you consider the times you asked and had to wait? Do you think of the hours of prayer, the convincing pleas you sent up, or the tears that you shed? Or do you simply accept that God does all things well, in His own timing? So, when you think of the many times that man has failed, you must appreciate the countless times that God has not. God may have asked you to wait, but He will come through, again. In His own time. Just wait. And have a rewarded day.

> *And it shall come to pass, that before they call, I will answer; and while they are yet speaking, I will hear. (Isaiah 65:24)*

What is something that you feel you have been waiting for God to do for you?

_____
_____
_____

Find at least two scripture references which speak about waiting on God. Copy these scriptures, and post them where you can see them each day. Repeat theses scriptures until they become your way of thinking. God will honor your patience.

Scripture reference 1.

_____
_____
_____

Scripture reference 2.

_____
_____
_____

If Jesus paid it all, why are you still bargaining for your inheritance? If He has the whole world in His hand, why are you begging for handouts? If the bread belongs to the children of God, why are you settling for crumbs? If the cattle on a thousand hills are His, why are you living in fear and not by faith? God has spoken, and the Word has gone forth into the world. "He who has begun a good work is about to fulfill it." Wait in expectancy, but live in the fulfillment of that expectation. "It is finished." Claim it. And have a fulfilled day.

> *Being confident of this very thing, that he which hath begun a good work in you will perform it until the day of Jesus Christ: (Philippians 1:6)*

What are three promises that you are believing God to fulfill in your life?

1. _____
2. _____
3. _____

What evidences will let you know when they have been accomplished?

When you spend your night worried about tomorrow, what does it accomplish? There is no problem that worry can solve, and there is none that Jesus can't. Instead of worrying about what is to be, or what might never be, worry about what you are giving the Savior to take care of. Be it big or small, He can handle it. Leave for tomorrow the issues of tomorrow, and hand the issues of today over to the master. Trust Him that he can handle what seems impossible. And have a stress-free day

> *Take therefore no thought for the morrow: for the morrow shall take thought for the things of itself. Sufficient unto the day is the evil thereof. (Matthew 6:34)*

Make a list of all the things that you are worried about.

Take a few minutes in prayer and give them to God to handle. Write your prayer here in which you allow God to have control of all your worries.

_____
_____
_____
_____

Determine in your mind that you are not staying where you are. You are in the midst of your storm? He will lead you to still waters. You are on your journey with stressors and oppressors? He will lead you to the path of righteousness. You are going through your valley of darkness and death? He is with you. You are grieved and heavy laden? His rod and staff are there to comfort you. It doesn't matter where you are right now. He is there to bring you through. Don't determine to stay where you are when God has already made a place for you on Victory Mountain. It's time to move out of loss and want and relocate to deliverance and Blessings. It is God's will concerning you. Upgrade. And have an elevated day

> *The Lord is my shepherd; I shall not want. He maketh me to lie down in green pastures: he leadeth me beside the still waters. He restoreth my soul: he leadeth me in the paths of righteousness for his name's sake. Yea, though I walk through the valley of the shadow of death, I will fear no evil: for thou art with me; thy rod and thy staff they comfort me. (Psalm 23:1, 2, 3, 4)*

What is one situation of those noted above that you are facing?

_____
_____
_____
_____

How can you "upgrade" your circumstance today?

_____
_____
_____
_____

As you face the struggles of work and family today, remember to focus on your purpose. Whatever you are asked you do, or whatever you feel the need to do, let it be done with purpose. Whether you are commended or recommended, let your purpose be the driving force behind your actions. If no one sees your sacrifice, God does. And He will be the ultimate rewarder. So, seek to please Him today as you fulfill your purpose. And have a motivated day

> *So then, whether you eat or drink, or whatever you may do, do all for the honor and glory of God. (1 Corinthians 10:31) (AMPV)*

What is your purpose in life?

_____
_____
_____
_____

What are you doing to fulfill that purpose and to bring honor to Christ?

_____
_____
_____
_____

Be chaste in both your approach to and departure from any confrontation today. This means that your morals will be pure. You will not seek to exalt self. You will not seek to lessen others. If you must be angry, let it be righteous anger. Give no opening for the enemy to enter. Just as a soft answer turns away wrath, so too does a chaste and humble spirit. Purity is of God, and is of the body, mind, and Spirit. So be an example of the believer in purity, so that God may be glorified. And have a holy day.

> *Be thou an example of the believers, in word, in conversation, in charity, in spirit, in faith, in purity. (1 Timothy 4:12)*

What plan do you have in place to avoid confrontation today?
___
___
___
___

If you must face a confrontation, how will you ensure that God is glorified by the outcome?
___
___
___
___
___
___

So, it's the day of "love," and persons are confessing or professing love. Those who never felt it, suddenly do. Those who never said it, suddenly can. Those who never heard it, unexpectedly will. And those who genuinely love will be silent, because love is not something that is said; it is something that is done. Anyone can speak love, but only those who know the meaning of sacrifice can do love. Christ "loved" us so much, that He "gave" His life to show us. That is doing love. So, unless you can do it, don't say it. Live love. And have an appreciative day

> *For God so loved the world, He gave His only begotten son. That whosoever believeth in Him should not perish, but have eternal life. (John 3:16)*

Find someone to share love with today.

Record the experience.

_____
_____
_____
_____
_____
_____

Do you know what the scripture means when it speaks about being unequally yoked? Do you immediately think of the good girl -- bad boy scenario? Do you imagine a fine minister and his ghetto-style girl? Or do you visualize the evangelist in her broad hat while her husband is at home on the couch with the remote or a bottle? Well here's the real truth. You could both be in the pulpit and be unequally yoked. You could both be on the prayer team and be unequally yoked. It's not about the place where you worship that makes it unequal. It's about the level of worship and commitment in the relationship. It's about the support for the ministry and the constant reminders they give which helps to keep your faith and focus in and on God. Not every inequality is reason for disqualification. Stay the course and see what God will do. And have a divinely-united day.

> *Be ye not unequally yoked together with unbelievers: for what fellowship hath righteousness with unrighteousness? and what communion hath light with darkness? (2 Corinthians 6:14)*

What is your understanding of "being unequally yoked"?

_____
_____
_____
_____

What can you do in your personal relationships to equalize the yoke/s that you are sharing?

_____
_____
_____
_____

What is an "if" question? If you haven't had an "if" question sent your way, one is coming soon. He's asking, "If you trust me, why do you question my actions? If you love me, why do you not show it, or say it? If you are committed to me, why are you holding yourself back?" These are the "if" questions that you need to be on the lookout for. And when Christ asks these questions, "if" you can't answer them, as with any real relationship, you need to reevaluate. If Christ loved you enough to die for you, why can't you commit to Him, trust Him, and tell Him how you feel? He's waiting to hear from your heart. But as in any real relationship, he won't wait forever. Be warned. And have an aware day.

To day if ye will hear his voice, harden not your hearts, as in the provocation. (Hebrews 3:15)

What is an "if" question that you know God is asking you?

_____
_____
_____
_____

What is your answer?

_____
_____
_____
_____

If your response included an excuse, what do you need to do to change from excuses to action?

_____
_____
_____
_____

Whenever you get frustrated enough to quit, remember why you started. If you haven't reached that goal you were aiming for, it's too soon to stop. A mountain is never scaled by starting at the top. And a valley is never crossed by standing on the mountain looking down. You have to be in it to win. If Jesus had stopped at the foot of Mount Calvary, where would you be today? Keep climbing. The mountain top is in view, and the other side of the valley is just around the corner. You will make it if you don't stop now. Press on. And have a determined day.

> *The LORD God is my strength, and he will make my feet like hinds' feet, and he will make me to walk upon mine high places. (Habakkuk 3:19)*

What is it that you are planning on quitting, giving up, or walking away from?

_____

_____

_____

Have you tried all avenues to accomplish your goal?

Who are some persons who you can reach out to that may be able to help you in your journey?

Names:

1.

2.

3.

Choose one person from your list and call him or her up. Tell him/her what you are attempting and ask for some suggestions.

Suggestions:

_____

_____

_____

Now, follow through.

Repeat as needed.

If you are still stuck on the love issue, remember this. Love is an action word. Love says, and then does what it says. Love remembers. Love forgives. Love reaches out. Love responds. Love waits. Love progresses. Love stays awake and aware. Love grows and flourishes. Love sacrifices. Love does not fade. If there are only words, but no actions, beware. It's likely to be the reflection of what was, not what is. Christ is love. He acted on His word. He died so that you might live. He is the reality of what love is. So learn to act. Learn to love. And have a love-filled day.

> *Love suffers long and is kind; love does not envy; love does not parade itself, is not puffed up; does not behave rudely, does not seek its own, is not provoked, thinks no evil; does not rejoice in iniquity, but rejoices in the truth; bears all things, believes all things, hopes all things, endures all things. (1 Corinthians 13:4, 5, 6, 7) (NKJV)*

Return to the last reading on love. Did you find someone to share your love with?

Describe what that experience was like and how you feel about it.

_____

_____

_____

_____

If you still haven't found someone to share love with, look around you. When you have found that someone to reach out to, to give hope to, record your experience and response above.

If you already shared love, do it again. There is no limit to giving of love.

It's been said before, but it must be said again. Whether by choice or necessity, you have to act. When someone is hurting, you have to respond with a word of comfort. When someone is in need, you have to respond with a helping hand. When someone is lost, you have to offer to show them the way. Jesus said that this is how we show that we are His disciples. It doesn't matter if he or she is the least among you. They need the hand of love in order to survive. Your hand. So help someone up who has fallen. And have a blessing day.

> *By this shall all men know that ye are my disciples, if ye have love one to another. (John 13:35)*

What will you do to bless someone today?

_____

_____

_____

_____

How will you accomplish this in a way that you are not the one receiving the glory, but God is?

_____

_____

_____

_____

When you look in the mirror, stop looking for the person people expect you to be. Look at the you who really hides inside. Whether you are happy with what you see or not, it's your true reflection. What you allow others to make you look for is for their satisfaction, not for your happiness. Stop trying to be, and accept that you are. The only one who you need to satisfy is Christ, and He already sees you as you will be in Him. Smile. And have a self-affirming day.

> *I will praise thee; for I am fearfully and wonderfully made: marvellous are thy works; and that my soul knoweth right well. (Psalm 139:14)*

Starting today, spend five to ten minutes in the mirror just looking at yourself.

Who or what do you see?

_____
_____
_____

How familiar are you with the person looking back at you?

"I'm not sure that I know this person, because ...

_____
_____
_____

"I know this person very well, because...

_____
_____
_____

How happy are you with the person that you see? Why?

_____
_____
_____

BIBLE BITES

Is that your true self? Why or why not?

_____
_____
_____

What can you say to your reflection to align her with who you truly desire her to be? Review your previous affirmations.

_____
_____
_____
_____
_____

At this very moment, you are going through. You are under the weight of oppression and fear. You are struggling with the same weight that has so often beset you. You are facing that familiar mountain, and wondering how to overcome it, again. But God. Many are the afflictions of the righteous, but the Lord will deliver you out of them all. Remember, you've come too far to give up. Just wait on the Lord, and be of good courage. He will strengthen your heart. Hold on just a little longer. And have an unbeatable day.

> *Many are the afflictions of the righteous: but the Lord delivereth him out of them all. (Psalm 34:19)*
>
> *Wait on the Lord: be of good courage, and he shall strengthen thine heart: wait, I say, on the Lord. (Psalm 27:14)*

What do the two scripture references mean to you personally?

_____
_____
_____
_____

How will you face your challenges differently, know that these are the promises of God to those who wait on Him, and who suffer for the sake of righteousness?

_____
_____
_____
_____

There are some things that you are dealing with right now, that seem trivial to others. They don't understand your struggle nor your test. And why should they? It's your struggle, your test, your testimony. This is where the victim becomes the victor, and the needy becomes the needed. God will lift you up, and those who didn't understand your struggle will not understand your praise. But they'll see your glory. This is the promise of the Lord. So trust the process. And have a rejoicing day.

> *Humble yourselves in the sight of the Lord, and he shall lift you up. (James 4:10)*

What has God brought you through or out of that you can use to help someone in their struggle?

_____
_____
_____
_____

What medium can you use to share this testimony?

_____
_____
_____
_____

Go ahead. Let someone know that God has done it for you, and He will do it for them.

Sometimes the hardest decision you can make is to walk away. Walking away seems like failure; you can't handle it, you aren't good enough, you don't have what it takes. However, walking away really means that you are strong enough to quit, smart enough to know when you can't take any more, and proud enough to leave with dignity. Sin is the hardest thing to walk away from, so when you do, do it with the knowledge that you couldn't do any better than that. Let no one make you feel guilty for walking out on your hurt and disappointments; especially when you are walking towards Christ and better things. Be strong in the Lord. And have a liberated day.

> *For our light and momentary troubles are achieving for us an eternal glory that far outweighs them all. (2 Corinthians 4:17)*

> *Finally, my brethren, be strong in the Lord, and in the power of his might. (Ephesians 6:10)*

What do you need to walk away from today?

_____
_____
_____
_____

How will you do it with yourself intact? Write a plan for your exit speech. Be sure to clearly state your intent and reasons. Then provide a solution for those who you may be leaving behind. Ensure that your plan is sound and realistic.

_____
_____
_____
_____

To be responsible means to be response able. It means that you are able to answer when called upon to fulfill your response abilities. You are able to rise to the occasion and give an account of your actions. It means that you are able to give a response when your family is falling apart or hurting. Stop saying that you have responsibilities, when you are not able to respond. You who are called by Christ must remember that He is the example of how you must respond. Be available, able, and accountable. And have a responsive day.

> But if anyone does not provide for his relatives, and especially for members of his household, he has denied the faith and is worse than an unbeliever. (1 Timothy 5:8)

> Likewise, husbands, live with your wives in an understanding way, showing honor to the woman as the weaker vessel, since they are heirs with you of the grace of life, so that your prayers may not be hindered. (1 Peter 3:7)

> Bear one another's burdens, and so fulfill the law of Christ. (Galatians 6:2)

What are you responsible for?

1. _____

2.

3.

4.

5.

How "able" are you to respond to these tasks?

_____
_____
_____

What will you do to improve your "ability" to "respond" in an effective manner?

_____
_____
_____

So the journey is coming to an end. You've gotten a tan, mailed the postcards back home, and bought all those souvenirs. Now you're looking to make sure your travel documents are in order? Don't leave the most important things for last. Make sure you're ready to travel before you get carried away with proving you've been on a trip. That's why the scripture says to set your affections on things above, not on things of the earth. When you get caught up in the proving and miss the living, what do you have to show for it? Get yourself covered first, then live so others know you're going, but that they'll see you again one day. Life is too short to be unprepared for when the stay is over. So, be equipped. And have a secure day

> *Set your affection on things above, not on things on the earth. (Colossians 3:2)*

What would you need to "get in order" if you were to leave this world today? What are some natural and spiritual "loose ends" which need to be tied up before you go?

_____
_____
_____
_____

Don't allow distractions to dominate your life. Each time you stop the thing you just started, you're one more procrastination nearer to finishing nothing. Half done is also half undone, and almost did means you also didn't. Remember that the prize goes to the one who completes the race, not the one who almost finished. There are no heavenly rewards for those who almost made it in. So, set your focus, keep your focus, and run all. And have a determined day.

> *Do you not know that those who run in a race all run, but one receives the prize? Run in such a way that you may obtain it. (1 Corinthians 9:24)*

Today, refocus.

What is that thing which you started but have yet to complete?

_____
_____
_____
_____

What do you need to do to complete it?

_____
_____
_____
_____

Now, go do it.

What steps did you take today to complete your unfinished task?

1.
2.
3.
4.
5.

Just because the scripture says that "a soft answer turns away wrath," it doesn't mean that you have to say anything. What's the point of claiming that God fights your battles if you keep getting in the way? It's time to learn to be silent. A soft answer can have some harsh points and do much damage if not handled carefully. It might turn off anger, but it can still leave others hurt. So, let the Lord truly fight your battles, both verbal and physical. And have a recompensed day.

> *Submit yourselves therefore to God. Resist the devil, and he will flee from you. (James 4:7) (ESV)*

What battle do you need to step away from and leave to God?
_____
_____
_____
_____

What harsh words, spoken in a moment of anger, to you need to apologize for?
_____
_____
_____
_____

Today, begin to mend that relationship that has been damaged by your words and attitude.

At times the Lord uses others and situations to get your attention. You are so focused on life that He has to remind you that He is there. But sometimes, He will be silent. He will not answer, He will not send a storm, and He will not send a preacher. He will be silent. It doesn't mean He isn't speaking. It means that He is waiting for you to be silent. And in that moment of silence, you will find Him. He will minister to your spirit as you quietly wait. And He will restore your peace. Just listen. And have a refreshing day.

> *And, behold, the Lord passed by, and a great and strong wind rent the mountains, and brake in pieces the rocks before the Lord; but the Lord was not in the wind: and after the wind an earthquake; but the Lord was not in the earthquake: And after the earthquake a fire; but the Lord was not in the fire: and after the fire a still small voice. And it was so, when Elijah heard it, that he wrapped his face in his mantle, and went out, and stood in the entering in of the cave. And, behold, there came a voice unto him, and said, What doest thou here, Elijah? (1 Kings 19:11, 12, 13)*
>
> *Be still, and know that I am God: I will be exalted among the heathen, I will be exalted in the earth. (Psalm 46:10)*

When was the last time that you stayed silent to allow yourself to hear from God?

_____

_____

What is the "noise" that is getting in the way of you hearing from God?

_____

_____

_____

How can you quiet the noise so that the voice of God becomes dominant in your life?

_____

_____

_____

_____

Some decisions that you will have to make will be life changing. You will hurt, or you will hurt others. You will question those decisions, or others will question them for you. You will feel regret, or you will leave others with regrets. However, there comes a time when you have to decide. So it is with your eternal decision. Heaven or hell? It's up to you to decide. There are those who would rather see you suffer than be saved, beaten down than be blessed, the victim rather than the victor. So decide for yourself, because your decision is a matter of life and death. Choose wisely. And have an assured day.

> *For the wages of sin is death; but the gift of God is eternal life in Christ Jesus our Lord. (Romans 6:23)*
>
> *And if it seem evil unto you to serve the LORD, choose you this day whom ye will serve; whether the gods which your fathers served that were on the other side of the flood, or the gods of the Amorites, in whose land ye dwell: but as for me and my house, we will serve the LORD. (Joshua 24:15)*

What decision are you facing that needs your immediate attention?

_____

_____

_____

What do you need to do today to finalize that decision?

_____

_____

_____

_____

How will this positively impact your life? Or, what change will this bring about in your life?

_____

_____

_____

_____

Some questions are not meant to be answered, just like some decisions are not meant to be made. You have options and choices. You can opt to respond or choose to be silent. Just as there are some doors which read, "Do not open," and others which read, "push," or "pull," so it is with option and choice. It's up to you to follow the signs or make your own choice. Just realize that there are challenges to every option and consequences to every choice. And behind every closed door, there is a chance of danger or success, but you have to choose. Use wisdom. And have a decisive day.

> *See, I have set before thee this day life and good, and death and evil; (Deuteronomy 30:15)*
>
> *I call heaven and earth to record this day against you, [that] I have set before you life and death, blessing and cursing: therefore choose life, that both thou and thy seed may live: (Deuteronomy 30:19)*

What was the option that you went with yesterday?
_____
_____
_____

What was the most difficult obstacle that you were faced with?
_____
_____
_____

What were the results of facing this difficulty?
_____
_____
_____

What has this situation taught you about the way that you handle challenges?
_____
_____
_____

Consider this. Every word you speak is being listened to, recorded, and evaluated, and you are being held accountable. There is someone who is listening to you for their life's direction, healing, and salvation. Your words are never merely words; they are someone's comfort, peace, and safety. That's why you are cautioned to "Let no filthy communication come out of your mouth." "For out of the mouth, the heart speaketh." So be careful who you cause to falter, and be careful who you choose to praise. Someone is listening, and they keep good records. Speak cautiously. And have a responsible day.

> *Let no corrupt communication proceed out of your mouth, but that which is good to the use of edifying, that it may minister grace unto the hearers. (Ephesians 4:29)*

> *A good man out of the good treasure of his heart bringeth forth that which is good; and an evil man out of the evil treasure of his heart bringeth forth that which is evil: for of the abundance of the heart his mouth speaketh. (Luke 6:45)*

Write three or more phrases (negative and positive) that you often use.

_____

_____

_____

Think of a person for each phrase above, that is, or may be, influenced by what you say.

_____

_____

_____

How can you change or replace these phrases to positively, or more positively, impact others?

_____

_____

_____

_____

Over the next week, try to use your new phrases and note the results they have on others.

Have you ever been on the verge of a meltdown? You were tired, sad, frustrated, and lonely? You were sure that you were unloved, and maybe unlovable? You were close to giving up? And right at the moment, just as you said, "I can't do this anymore," just as you dared to tell God, "I'm sorry, but I've had enough," and just as you decided to call God on His promises, His assumed inattention, someone says something like, "God wants you to know that He loves you. He wants you to know that you are His child, and He has not forgotten you?" That's God. Today He wants you (yes, you) to know that He has not forgotten you. He is working on your situation. He does love you, and He will never let you down. Weeping may be your portion for a night, but joy awaits you in the morning. So dry those tears. And go have a reassuring day.

> *For his anger endureth but a moment; in his favour is life: weeping may endure for a night, but joy cometh in the morning. (Psalm 30:5)*

Write a short note to yourself as a reminder of God's promise to you of His constant presence.

Your Name:

_____

_____

_____

_____

Signed, God

Review your earlier affirmations and add two new statements to remind yourself of who you are in Christ.

_____

_____

_____

_____

Hard as it may be to believe, not every lie that is told to you is meant to deceive. While a lie is the misrepresentation of the truth, the truth is that some persons actually believe that what they are telling you is the truth. So even though you realize the information is wrong, and you could prove it if you had to, first, check for the truth behind the lie. Be sure that what is a lie to you isn't the other person's reality. Remember, the scripture says that "you" shall know the truth, and it shall make "you" free. It's not about proving the others wrong; it's about knowing what's right. So hold fast to your truth. And have an honest day.

And ye shall know the truth, and the truth shall make you free. (John 8:32)

Today, take time to truly listen to others as they tell their "truths." Refuse to pass judgment. Just listen. When you go into prayer, remember to ask God to allow you to discern the truth from the lie. Now, walk in your freedom, without judgment of others.

Have you ever watched someone laying bricks? The detailing that goes into making sure that each brick is cut just right is amazing. Each one must be the same size, depending on the design of the finished product. Edges must be even, so if one brick is damaged, it has to be recycled or cut to serve another purpose. The great brick layer, Christ, takes such care when He is building you. There are some surfaces in your design that are smooth, and some that may be chipped or damaged. That's why He needs to cut you at times, to ensure that everything fits together just right when the molding is over. So trust the master builder that He is working things out for your good. When you are finished, you will be worthy of carrying His seal, "Created in His image." So trust the cutting and molding process. And have a divinely-restructured day.

> *But he knoweth the way that I take: when he hath tried me, I shall come forth as gold. (Job 23:10)*

What is something that you need Christ to "perfect" in you?

_____
_____
_____
_____

How will you know when the work has been done?

_____
_____
_____
_____

Have you ever wanted something done, but you never moved to accomplish it? Was it ever done? No? To accomplish the possible and the impossible, you have to move. Movers soar, and movers grow. Nothing happens when you are standing still. That's why the scripture instructs us to be doers, not just hearers. Even Jesus was writing on the ground while He was hearing the accusations brought against the woman caught in adultery. He was doing something to prepare for her deliverance. What are you doing to prepare for yours? Stop stalling, and start moving. Remember that there is much to be accomplished, and time waits on no one. So get things moving. And have a productive day.

> *But be ye doers of the word, and not hearers only, deceiving your own selves. (James 1:22)*

Take thirty minutes today to just visualize the fulfilment of your plans for success.

Describe that vision and the accompanying feeling.

_____
_____
_____
_____

Take ten or more minutes each day and do one thing that will help you reach that goal.

Even if others betray you, don't betray yourself by becoming what they say about you. There are those who will set you up and watch while you walk into the trap. This is so that they can come along and be your hero. Your hero already did all that was needed to be done when He went to the cross and died for you. Don't believe every story, and don't cry at every tragedy. Your inner voice is there to alert you. So when they start talking, listen to your inner voice that's saying "walk away," and don't become their victim. You were born to be a victor. Never forget that. Live your true self. And have a victorious day.

> *Surely in vain the net is spread in the sight of any bird. (Proverbs 1:17)*
>
> *Being confident of this, that he who began a good work in you will carry it on to completion until the day of Christ Jesus. (Philippians 1:6) (NIV)*

As you go through your daily routine, pay attention to the things that you allow into your space and mind. Guard your mind and your spirit. Post a verse or affirmation where you can reference it, reminding yourself to be on guard today.

Write your verse or affirmation that you plan to post.

_____
_____
_____
_____

There is a voice rising up inside of you. It wants to be heard. It needs to be heard. Let the voice which has been silent for so long be free to declare, "By His stripes I am healed. The Son has set me free. Therefore, I am free indeed. And the weapons that have been formed against me, they shall no longer prosper." There is no need for others to declare your victory. Speak life into your own situation. Declare that the Lord has ordained your deliverance. And "It is finished." Go ahead and speak your healing. And have an affirmative day.

> Surely he hath borne our griefs, and carried our sorrows: yet we did esteem him stricken, smitten of God, and afflicted. But he was wounded for our transgressions, he was bruised for our iniquities: the chastisement of our peace was upon him; and with his stripes we are healed. (Isaiah 53:4, 5)

1. Speak life into your own situation. Make a declaration today that "By His stripes I am healed. The Son has set me free. Therefore, I am free indeed. And the weapons that have been formed against me, they shall no longer prosper."

   Repeat this as often as needed, until you see the evidence of what your faith declares.

2. Write your own scripture-based declaration that you repeat each day as a declaration of your faith.

_____

_____

_____

_____

How many times have you felt like you are only making it by your willpower? You wake up daily and will yourself out of bed. You will yourself out of the house. You will yourself though the day. Then you return home, and by mere willpower, you take care of your family responsibilities, and once again, job issues. Stop living by willpower, and start living by Christ power. The scripture states that the just shall live by faith, not by willpower. Have faith enough to believe that Christ has ordained all that you are facing and all that you will face in your daily life. When you know that He has taken care of even the simple act of getting you out of bed, why won't He take care of everything else? Trust Him on the little things, and watch Him work on the big. And have a Christ-directed day.

> *Behold, his soul which is lifted up is not upright in him: but the just shall live by his faith. (Habakkuk 2:4)*

> *For in him we live, and move, and have our being; as certain also of your own poets have said, For we are also his offspring. (Acts 17:28)*

What are you willing yourself to do today?
_____
_____
_____
_____

Make a faith statement that tells God how much you trust Him to be in control of all your situations today.
_____
_____
_____
_____

Now let Him be in control.

There is a big difference between welcoming someone and welcoming the Holy Spirit. When you welcome persons into your inner space, you are saying, "I know you, I've tried you, and I trust you." When you say, "Holy spirit I welcome you," you are saying, "I invite you to commune with me, I invite you to dwell in me, I invite you to teach me." However, when the Holy Spirit welcomes you, it means that there is something that the Holy Spirit wants to refine in you. You are being invited into His presence so that you may be comforted, strengthened, and edified. We can do nothing for the Holy Spirit, so welcoming Him in is simply realizing that you need Him most. So accept His invite and allow Him to make the difference in your life. And have a refined day.

> *And I will pray the Father, and he shall give you another Comforter, that he may abide with you for ever; (John 14:16)*
>
> *Howbeit when he, the Spirit of truth, is come, he will guide you into all truth: (John 16:13)*

Spend some time today basking in the presence of the Holy Spirit. Listen as He communes with you. As you listen, pay attention to the thoughts which are birthed.

Write as many of these thoughts out and review to see what the Lord has revealed to you in your moments of communion.

_____

_____

_____

_____

What do you need to address from what has been revealed?

_____

_____

_____

_____

Act on it immediately.

Stress has a way of weakening your body. It tires you, leaves you with stomach problems, raises your blood pressure, and adds on unnecessary weight. Yet you stress yourself every day. Sin has the same effects. It will drain your resources, cramp your spiritual life, raise your chances of eternal death, and keep you weighted down with earthly burdens. However, it's easier to get rid of sin than of stress. But when you get rid of your sin, stress will also go. Just let Jesus take away the thing that so easily besets you, and watch the stress roll away. When he changes your life around, He will change everything in your atmosphere around. So let Him take control and lift the unneeded weights. And have a relieved day.

> *Wherefore seeing we also are compassed about with so great a cloud of witnesses, let us lay aside every weight, and the sin which doth so easily beset us, and let us run with patience the race that is set before us. (Hebrews 12:1)*
>
> *Casting all your care upon him; for he careth for you. (1 Peter 5:7)*

What are some weights that you need to lay aside?
_____
_____
_____

What's stopping you from doing so?
_____
_____
_____

What will you do to lose those weights?
_____
_____
_____
_____

Do it.

There are hundreds of fruits in the world, and they all contain different elements which serve different purposes. There are some persons who can use some of these fruits, but others who cannot. Then, there are some who have access to these fruits, but others who do not. Then there is the fruit of the Spirit. This one fruit contains only nine elements, but it can be used by all and is accessible to every individual. It is free and can be given away without the giver suffering loss or want. Just imagine the benefits of love, joy, peace, longsuffering, gentleness, goodness, faith, meekness, and temperance. If you are ever in need of strength, hope, comfort, or acceptance, just try the fruit of the Spirit, and you will be made whole. So feast on His fruit. And have a Spirit-filled day.

> *But the fruit of the Spirit is love, joy, peace, longsuffering, gentleness, goodness, faith, meekness, temperance: against such there is no law. (Galatians 5:22, 23)*

What are you lacking of the "Fruit of the Spirit"?

_____

_____

_____

_____

Write a prayer asking God to increase that "fruit" in you, then put it into action. Push through, even when it seems that you are still lacking. The more you use a thing, the more of it you experience.

_____

_____

_____

_____

How many keys do you have which you actually use? Are they all for your house, or job, or other family members' homes? You often walk around with keys that aren't yours, or that are no longer functional. Maybe you are hoping that someday, you'll find out where that key fits? Remember. Not every person or everything in your life serves a purpose, just as not every key has a lock that it stills fits. Or maybe, the purpose has been fulfilled, and it's time to let them go. Don't hold on to extra keys, or those who no longer fit the hole they were once fitting in to. Maybe the lock is worn, or has been changed. Whatever the reason, if it no longer fits, don't force it. The scripture states that you must put off the old man in order for the new man to exist. So lose those dysfunctional keys that no longer serve a purpose and upgrade to a new security system in Jesus. He will fit every locked door in your life. No keys required. Let Him open new doors for you. And have a secured day.

> *That ye put off concerning the former conversation the old man, which is corrupt according to the deceitful lusts; And be renewed in the spirit of your mind; And that ye put on the new man, which after God is created in righteousness and true holiness. (Ephesians 4:22, 23, 24)*

Take an inventory today:

How many unnecessary keys are you holding on to? They once served a purpose, so you keep holding on? Today, determine to discard those keys. Make it intentional.

Who or what are you holding on to that no longer fits your life?

_____
_____
_____
_____
_____
_____
_____

Let them go. Ask God for the way, and He will do it.

Do you know that God has a sense of humor? Not the "crack a joke and wait for the punch line," type of humor. It's the "you think you are going to go your own way, do your own thing, but you're not," type of humor. Do you know that He will permit you to make your own choice, choose your own path, but He'll use your decision to teach you that He is God? Don't think for a minute that you can put one over on Him. He is all knowing, all present, and all powerful. When you have done all that you plan, He will still be waiting there for you to accept that He is God. He will not be mocked. So stop trying to have the last laugh on God, and realize that He will have His way, with or without you. So, get serious for, and about your walk with God. And have a focused day.

> *Be not deceived; God is not mocked: for whatsoever a man soweth, that shall he also reap. For he that soweth to his flesh shall of the flesh reap corruption; but he that soweth to the Spirit shall of the Spirit reap life everlasting. (Galatians 6:7, 8)*

Today, think of that "Thing" that you are intent on doing, even when your spirit is advising against it.

What will you gain by pursuing this course of action?

_____
_____
_____
_____

If it will not bring honor to God, walk away from it. Remember, God will get the glory with or without you.

When God has called you to His service, it doesn't mean that you are special or unique. It means that He has a job that you have been purposed to do. Never allow the call to become your focus. Although there is no one else who can fulfill your purpose, there are many who can complete your job. Never forget that you are called to serve, not to be served. You are called to action, not to be the act. Keep your focus and intent on Christ and His glory, and He will keep you on the journey to your glory. It's about Him after all. Put Him first. And have a humble day.

> And lest I should be exalted above measure through the abundance of the revelations, there was given to me a thorn in the flesh, the messenger of Satan to buffet me, lest I should be exalted above measure. (2 Corinthians 12:7)

> For I say, through the grace given unto me, to every man that is among you, not to think of himself more highly than he ought to think; but to think soberly, according as God hath dealt to every man the measure of faith. (Romans 12:3)

What prideful-stance are you holding onto today?

_____
_____
_____
_____

What would it mean to you is you humbled yourself in that situation? What would it look like? Will God be glorified?

_____
_____
_____
_____

Remember, "Pride comes before a fall."

When the phone rings, do you look to see the number? If it's unknown, you have to make a decision. Answer or ignore? What if it's someone you promised never to talk to again? You run the risk of opening old wounds, and stirring up old feelings. What if you aren't ready to face that person? But what if it's some long lost friend you've been hoping to contact, or someone in your inner circle who needs you right away? You weren't expecting the call, but you don't want to miss them. What if it was the Lord on the line, calling to check that you were ok, or ready to go with Him? Sometimes you have to run the risk of being hurt so that you don't miss your blessing. You never know when the Lord will call, so the important thing is to be ready to answer. It will not always be the old familiar number, and it won't necessarily be "in the morning" when He calls. It will be when you least expect it, so you must be ready to answer. Be prepared. And have a receptive day.

> *Therefore be ye also ready: for in such an hour as ye think not the Son of man cometh. (Matthew 24:44)*

Are you ready if Christ were to call you up on the telephone today?

_____
_____
_____

What would be the topic/s of your conversation?

_____
_____
_____
_____

What would you answer if asked to give an account of your time here on earth?

_____
_____
_____
_____

Be prepared.

When you leave home today, you will be carrying a bag. In that bag will be all the things you need to get through your day. There will be some things that are heavy and some that are light. It's your bag, however, so you have to handle it. Don't allow anyone to add to your bag with their baggage. Don't let the anger, frustration, and hate that they are carrying become a part of your weight. All your peace, contentment, and happiness will become bent and misshaped. Don't allow them to empty your bag to fill it with their load. Carry your own with care, secure it, and keep a careful watch on it. Guard your heart, your mind, and your spirit. And have an unburdened day.

> *Above everything else guard your heart, because from it flow the springs of life. (Proverbs 4:23) (ISV)*
>
> *And the peace of God, which passeth all understanding, shall keep your hearts and minds through Christ Jesus. (Philippians 4:7)*

What are you carrying in your bag of cares and concern?
_____
_____
_____

What are some things that you are willing to carry in your bag for others?
_____
_____
_____

If you are neither willing, nor able, let that person know. Write what you need to say to ensure that he or she knows that you cannot help them. Remember, be loving, but firm.
_____
_____
_____
_____

Then turn your bag over to Jesus and let Him take your burden away.

When you finally decide to praise God, do it with all that is in you. Do it as if there is nothing more important. Do it as if there is no one more important. Praise Him as if your life depended on it. When you praise God, you open the way for worship to happen. When you worship Him in Spirit and in truth, you open the door for miracles to happen. When you praise God, you strengthen the relationship that exists between you and God. And that relationship is all that matters when you are ready to worship. So praise Him as if there is nothing else worth doing. And as you lift Him up, He will show up to fellowship with you. So worship Him with all that you are. And have a reverence-filled day.

> *Serve the Lord with gladness! Come into his presence with singing! (Psalm 100:2)*
>
> *Let everything that has breath praise the Lord! Praise the Lord! (Psalm 150:6)*
>
> *God is spirit, and those who worship him must worship in spirit and truth. (John 4:24)*

Write a song of "true praise" to God. Let your song reflect all that He has done for you and all that you appreciate Him for. When complete, sing your song aloud. "Make a joyful noise unto the Lord."

_____
_____
_____
_____

Whatever it takes, hold on to your sanctity. Hold on to your anointing. Hold on to your gift. There are those who are assigned to you, some to support your vision, and some to derail it. Hold fast to that which has been given to you by the laying on of hands and by the Holy Spirit. Prayers have been sent up and are recorded on your behalf. Refuse to allow the enemy's assignment to be your breaking point. Instead, allow the Master's assignments to be your breakthrough. Stay focused. Hold fast to your anointing. And have a fortified day.

> *Wherefore I put thee in remembrance that thou stir up the gift of God, which is in thee by the putting on of my hands. (2 Timothy 1:6)*

> *But the anointing which ye have received of him abideth in you, and ye need not that any man teach you: but as the same anointing teacheth you of all things, and is truth, and is no lie, and even as it hath taught you, ye shall abide in him. (1 John 2:27)*

Make a commitment today to hold fast to your faith.

Write an affirmation that you will not be moved.

_____

_____

_____

_____

As you go through the day, repeat over and over your affirmation that you will not let the enemy triumph over your praise.

If crying all the time solved every problem, would you cry all the time? No. Because, even crying becomes tiring after a while, and you realize that it doesn't usually get results. So when you get tired of wet cheeks and red eyes, try bent knees and a sincere heart. Tears are a language that God understands, but prayers are the keys to open locked doors. And while you are on your bended knees calling out to God from a sincere heart, He will be on your case, finalizing the plans to your deliverance. So cry less and pray more. And have an unbeatable day.

> *In my distress I called upon the LORD, and cried unto my God: he heard my voice out of his temple, and my cry came before him, even into his ears. (Psalm 18:6)*

> *In my distress I cried unto the Lord, and he heard me. (Psalm 120:1)*

Starting today, for one week, make the effort not to cry about your situation. Do not complain. Do not tell others about it.

Pray about it instead. Don't "cry" to God. Call out to Him. Tell Him what you specifically desire. On the

There's always going to be someone who rubs you the wrong way. But before you lose your cool, ask yourself, "What is this person's place in my life?" If you think he is a means of your survival, and you feel the need to hold on to him, then just pray. If on the other hand, you can do without her, then just pray for her and let her go. The solution is always to pray. The scripture says to pray for those who use you. So, whether you need them or not, pray for them. The more you pray, the easier it will be to forgive and love. And prayer sets the one who prays free. So just pray. And have a liberated day.

> *But I say unto you, Love your enemies, bless them that curse you, do good to them that hate you, and pray for them which despitefully use you, and persecute you; (Matthew 5:44)*
>
> *And whenever you stand praying, forgive, if you have anything against anyone, so that your Father also who is in heaven may forgive you your trespasses." (Mark 11:25)*

Who is that someone whom you cannot walk away from? What do you need to ask of God on their behalf so that your relationship may improve?

_____

_____

_____

_____

Who is that someone whom you need to pray out of your life? What do you need to tell God so that He will know what you truly want in this situation?

_____

_____

_____

_____

In order for you to be acceptably happy, you have to be able to strike a balance between needs and wants. You want to have friends, but you need to be there for your family. You want to put your family first, but you need to take care of yourself. You want to make sure you look out for yourself, but you need to focus on the job. You want to give your job all the attention it deserves, but you need to be happy. You want to be happy, but for that to happen, you need to know that Christ comes first. No matter what you want, to be really balanced, you need to start with Christ. He will supply all your needs, so that you will want for nothing. So put Him first. And have a satisfying day.

> *But my God shall supply all your need according to His riches in glory by Christ Jesus. (Philippians 4:19)*

> *But seek ye first the kingdom of God, and His righteousness; and all these things shall be added unto you. (Matthew 6:33)*

Make a list of at least five "needs", not wants.

1. _____
2. _____
3. _____
4. _____
5. _____
6. _____
7. _____
8. _____
9. _____
10. _____

How many of these can be met without having the peace of Christ in your heart?

_____
_____
_____

Now take the others that are stills "needs" and allow God the control to fulfill His plans that He has for you. In giving up control, you will find that all things that you need will be fulfilled.

If you think being victorious means walking away from the fight without a scratch, think again. To be victorious, you had to have been in the fight. You had to have taken a few punches, been down to your knees, thought you couldn't hold on any longer, and then you got up. To be victorious means that your hands got dirty, your back was hurt, your knees were buckling, but you kept pushing. Unless you've been pushed to your limit and realized that if it had not been for the Lord on your side, the enemy would have swallowed you up, you can't say you have the victory. To be victorious, you first had to be a victim. So stop complaining about the scratches, and get back into the fight. Your Captain is able to win you the victory. Stand fast. And have an overcoming day.

> *If it had not been the LORD who was on our side, now may Israel say; If it had not been the LORD who was on our side, when men rose up against us: Then they had swallowed us up quick ... (Psalm 124:1, 2, 3)*

> *The Lord of host is with us; the God of Jacob is our refuge. (Psalm 46:11)*

Are you a victim or a victor?

_____

What is your testimony about the scars that you have?

_____
_____
_____

If you have no scars, what do you have to complain about?

_____
_____
_____

If you do have scars, how are you using your battling experience to help others to grow?

_____
_____
_____

With all the bad news you are reading or hearing about, you might be tempted to worry. You begin to wonder if you are safe, or if those you love are safe. You find yourself checking behind you to be sure you locked the doors and fastened the windows. You check in with loved ones to be comforted when you hear that all is well. Yet, you give little attention to your safety in Jesus. You neglect to check in with Him to be assured that He hasn't been left outside that locked door. Don't get so wrapped up in fearing him who can destroy the body. Pay attention instead to Him who can destroy both the body and soul. For in Him is your safety and security. Reverence Him. And have a worry-free day.

> *Ye are of God, little children, and have overcome them: because greater is He that is in you, than he that is in the world. (1 John 4:4)*
>
> *And fear not them which kill the body, but are not able to kill the soul: but rather fear him which is able to destroy both soul and body in hell. (Matthew 10:28)*

What are you most worried with, or concerned about, today?
_____
_____
_____

Which of your fears can you control?
_____
_____
_____

If you can change a situation, do so. If you cannot, then remember that "God has not given you the fear spirit. He has provided you with a sober mind and with power. Use that power to speak peace to your spirit.

Note to self:
_____
_____
_____
_____

Sometimes your excuse for why you are the way you are, or why you do the things you do is that "God isn't finished with me yet." So what are you waiting for Him to still do? He saved you, sanctified you, called you, and appointed you. But He's not done with you yet? When God does a job, He does it well and completely. There are no loose strings to be cut or to be tied off. So instead of blaming God for how you are, maybe you need to be thanking Him, that in spite of all your flaws and inconsistencies, He loves you enough to not give up on you. The job was already done. So stop procrastinating and be ye holy, even as Jesus is holy. And have a sanctified day.

> *But as he which hath called you is holy, so be ye holy in all manner of conversation; Because it is written, Be ye holy; for I am holy. (1 Peter 1:15, 16)*
>
> *Being confident of this very thing, that He which hath begun a good work in you will perform it until the day of Jesus Christ: (Philippians 1:6)*

What are you still waiting for God to do in your life for you to be whom He has called you to be?

_____
_____
_____
_____

What are you "blaming" Him for, or, what has He "failed" to do in your life?

_____
_____
_____
_____

Stop your procrastination and make the changes which "you" need to make. God has already done His part. It's up to you to do yours.

One of the easiest ways to handle difficult situations or persons is to step back. Find a way to see the situation through the eyes of God, and see the person through the eyes of love. Never try to handle situations or persons from the eyes of what's right. What's right does not work for everything or everyone. But God and His love covers a multitude of evil, works for all that is right, and fixes all that is wrong. So love as if it were God you were seeing, and that will make anything or anyone easy to love. Love with the love that comes from God. And have an accepting day.

> *Above all, love each other deeply, because love covers over a multitude of sins. (1 Peter 4:8) (NIV)*

Today, step back from that situation or person.

Tell yourself, "This is not personal. This will be a means of God getting the glory."

Then, respond from a place of Godly love.

How did that turn out?

_____
_____
_____
_____
_____
_____
_____

What is your fear? If you fear losing someone, you are going to spend your time pushing them away, just so that you won't hurt when they go. If you fear success, you will do everything possible to sabotage your goals, just so that you can say, "I knew I couldn't do it." If you fear the unknown, you will never seek knowledge, just so you can say, "I didn't know." However, fear is not of God. He has given you a spirit of power, and that power says that anything is possible. Remember that FEAR means "Faith Expressed Alters Reality." So challenge yourself to change your reality. Believe that you can do all things through Christ. And have a courageous day.

> *For God hath not given us the spirit of fear; but of power, and of love, and of a sound mind. (2 Timothy 1:7)*

> *I can do all things through Christ which strengtheneth me. (Philippians 4:13)*

What is your fear?

_____

_____

_____

Fear is a concept, and it is of the mind. It can be changed, as any other concept may be changed.

Today, extend your faith and alter your reality.

Day after day, disappointments arise. Persons you trusted are the ones turning on you, pointing at you, shaking their heads in hopes of your fall. Plans are not working out as you hoped. Even the family members you helped are letting you down. But let them celebrate your temporary struggle. You know their end, don't you? The scripture tells us that He will make your enemies your footstool. Don't let one disappointment cause you to lose your promise of a footstool. Whatever the disappointments, don't give up. Tell every disappointment, "God got this." He does. Trust Him. And have a rewarding day.

> *For I was envious at the foolish, when I saw the prosperity of the wicked. Until I went into the sanctuary of God, then understood I their end. (Psalm 73:3, 17)*

What is that one disappointment which you are still stuck on? Why?

_____
_____
_____
_____

Let it go. There is little to gain from holding on to past hurts. There are some things which must occur and people who must hurt you so that you might become free to receive what God has waiting for you. Let the past go.

Sometimes you get upset about something someone said, did, or didn't do. You may raise your voice and say things that you later regret. And while the Bible says that we should be angry and sin not, you have to be careful not to abuse that God given right. Be angry only if it will solve the situation or right a wrong. Be angry with a godly anger. Don't say something that you know is intended to hurt someone just because you were hurt. Learn to love in spite of the anger, and remember that you are accountable for what comes out of the mouth. Speak wisely. And have a self-controlled day.

> *Set a watch, O LORD, before my mouth; keep the door of my lips. (Psalms 141:3)*

> *A soft answer turneth away wrath: but grievous words stir up anger. (Proverbs 15:1)*

Today, before you say what comes to the tip of your tongue, ask yourself, "Will this bring honor to God?" And, "Will I feel better about this situation and myself, after I have said this?" If either answer is "No," don't say it.

You've been reading the Word, finding comfort among the pages, been encouraged, and edified. You've been chastised and constrained by the power of the doctrine. Yet, suddenly, it's no longer working for you? You think that times have changed and what applied to you before, no longer applies today? Times have changed, yes. You have changed, yes. But God's word abideth forever. The scripture tells us that God cannot lie, because He is not man. Yet you opt to believe man about what God "really" meant, rather than believe what God has said and is still saying. God will not go back on His word, and He will not compromise to accommodate your changing up on Him. Let it be clear, he that adds to the word, or takes away from the word, will be called to give an account for daring to change God's word. Be warned. And have a thoughtful day.

> *God is not a man, that he should lie; neither the son of man, that he should repent: hath he said, and shall he not do it? or hath he spoken, and shall he not make it good? (Numbers 23:19)*
>
> *Heaven and earth shall pass away, but my words shall not pass away. (Matthew 24:35)*

What is something in the "Word" that you are being challenged on?

Scripture:

_____

_____

_____

_____

How will this change your faith or your beliefs about God?

_____

_____

_____

_____

Are you willing to risk your salvation by believing that God has changed His mind about what He requires?

Remember, God is holy, and he requires holiness of those who "trust" Him.

With tears in your eyes, and with sorrow in your heart, you learn that eventually, you have to let go. Let go of those you love, those whom you trusted, and those you depended on. Let go of those things that so easily beset you. Let go of those things which are behind, and those weights that are too heavy for you to carry alone. Just let go and see how light your load will become. Don't stay burdened out of comfort. It's time to become uncomfortable enough to let go and let God. The price was paid so that you need no longer be a slave to circumstances. Drop off the past, move on to better. And have a redeemed day.

> *Knowing this, that our old man is crucified with him, that the body of sin might be destroyed, that henceforth we should not serve sin. (Romans 6:6)*

What are you letting go of today?

1. _____
2. _____
3. _____
4. _____
5. _____

What are you going to pick up instead that will move you to a deeper relationship in Christ?

1. _____
2. _____
3. _____
4. _____
5. _____

With every new realization there comes an opportunity to either grow or not. You can choose to realize your shortcomings, or you can choose arrogance. You can choose to be honest, or you can choose to be unworthy of trust. You can choose to be approachable, or you can remain aloof. It's up to you to change your life for the positive or allow the negative to rule. Just realize that every man in Christ is a new creature. The old has to go when the nature of Christ takes over. So if you realize you have a problem, the fault is not in the power of Christ's blood. It's in you. Remember, realization is there to help you become who Christ knows you can be, not who you are. So act on the realization that it's time to grow. And have a fruitful day.

> *Therefore if any man be in Christ, he is a new creature: old things are passed away; behold, all things are become new. (2 Corinthians 5:17)*

What are two things which you will work to change in your attitude today?

1. _____
2. _____

What steps do you need to take to complete these changes?

1. _____
2. _____

With each change, reward yourself. Give yourself a star or sticker. See how many you can collect as you work on self-improving.

If you are still searching for true love, will you know when you find it? Will it be the fast beating of your heart, the stars in your eyes, the smile from ear to ear? How will you know that the other person feels the same? What will they have to do to prove that they really love you? Must they willingly give up family, leave their home land, face the jeers and insults of those who hate you? What will they have to sacrifice? Will they need to be ready to die for you? Will these be the evidences of true love? Will this be enough? This is the life that Jesus chose to prove that He loves you, and He asks for only one thing in return. Trust. No fast heartbeat, no stars in the eyes, no grin from ear to ear. As with any relationship that will survive, He asks you simply to trust Him. So if that's too much to give to prove that you love Him, what is your measure of true love? Today, recognize the true love that was displayed on the cross. And have a love-filled day.

> *Ephesians 2:4-5 But God, who is rich in mercy, for his great love wherewith he loved us, even when we were dead in sins, hath quickened us together with Christ, (by grace ye are saved;) (Ephesians 2:4, 5)*

> *In this was manifested the love of God toward us, because that God sent his only begotten Son into the world, that we might live through him. Herein is love, not that we loved God, but that he loved us, and sent his Son to be the propitiation for our sins. (1 John 4:9, 10, 11)*

What is your measure of true love?

_____

_____

_____

_____

What are five things that God has done for you which proves His love for you?

1. _____

2. _____

3. _____

4. _____

5. _____

What have you done to show your love for God?

_____
_____
_____
_____

Act on changing your evidence if you are uncomfortable with your response to the last question. If you are comfortable with your response, keep it up.

Do you know what a faith walk is? It's a journey you take by faith alone. It's going out into the storm with the knowledge that the lightning is dangerous, but the assurance that it won't strike you. It's going to the edge of the ocean with the knowledge that the waves are rough, but the assurance that they will not overtake you. It's standing on the mountain top with the knowledge that the fall down is steep, but with the assurance that He will catch you when you fall. A faith walk requires two things; knowledge and assurance. You know that the journey will be long, but you are assured that you will not faint. The important thing is to know who is going with you on your journey. With God leading, and goodness and mercy following, you'll make it safely to your destination. So step out by faith. And have a confidence-filled day.

> *Yea, though I walk through the valley of the shadow of death, I will fear no evil: for thou art with me; thy rod and thy staff they comfort me. (Psalm 23:4)*

> *When thou passest through the waters, I will be with thee; and through the rivers, they shall not overflow thee: when thou walkest through the fire, thou shalt not be burned; neither shall the flame kindle upon thee. (Isaiah 43:2)*

What will your faith walk require of you today?

_____
_____
_____

Are you prepared for the journey? Are you ready to let go and allow God to catch you? Why not?

_____
_____
_____

If not, spend some time before God, asking Him to build up or strengthen your faith that it fails not.

"Dear God…
_____
_____
_____

Before you go on an interview, you check to be sure that your resume is in order. You have all your experiences clearly listed, because that's what determines how believable you will be. You make sure that everything you've done in that field is at the top, in order of time spent building your abilities. It will be the same with Jesus. He will want to know what you did for Him in reference to promoting His kingdom. It won't be about the hours spent sitting in the pews, but the time given to prayer, worship, and service. It's important to have something to declare that you have honestly done, and He won't take any fake references. So get your life lined up to reflect the resume you're presenting. And have an acceptable day.

> *So then every one of us shall give account of himself to God. (Romans 14:12)*
>
> *For we must all appear before the judgment seat of Christ; that every one may receive the things done in his body, according to that he hath done, whether it be good or bad. (2 Corinthians 5:10)*

What category do you need to check and change, or adjust, in your resume for the kingdom?

_____

_____

_____

Is there anything that you can add to your resume which will reflect the time you have spent in the service of building God's kingdom?

_____

_____

_____

What can you do to improve your resume?

_____

_____

_____

_____

Now go do it.

Do you have any friends who have been there for you even when you were not there for them? Did they support your efforts, even when you rejected their advice? Were they willing to defend you, even when you denied them? Did they lay their reputations on the line even when they knew you could not be trusted to stay true to your word? No? That's what's so amazing about the love of God. In spite of your faults and failures, in spite of your inconsistencies, and in spite of your rejection of His grace and mercy, Jesus still loves you, will support you, will defend you, will come through for you, and even wants to be your friend. He is still thinking of you, in spite of it all. So give Him a call. And have a supportive day.

> *But God demonstrates his own love for us in this: While we were still sinners, Christ died for us. (Romans 5:8) (NIV)*

In what different ways or situations has Christ shown you that He is there for you?

_____
_____
_____
_____

Do you ever talk to yourself? Of course you do. But do you have a "real" conversation where you chastise yourself, berate yourself, beat yourself up? Do you remind yourself of the things you did that you shouldn't have done, the things you said that should not have been said? Do you tell yourself that you've done too much wrong to ever make things right? Then it's time to rewrite the script. It's time to tell yourself that you are forgiven. You are free from the past and redeemed to a new status. You are loved, and in Christ, all things can be made right. So the next time you start that conversation with your other self, tell him or her that you are no longer who you were. You are a child of God, a peculiar person, and royalty. That will be enough. Speak well of yourself and to yourself. And have a self-affirming day.

> *But ye are a chosen generation, a royal priesthood, an holy nation, a peculiar people; that ye should shew forth the praises of him who hath called you out of darkness into his marvellous light: (1 Peter 2:9)*

Write a memo-to-self, reminding yourself of whom you are in Christ. Post this memo where you can see it and reaffirm these truths daily.

"Dear _____

_____

_____

_____

_____

There's a song that asks, "Do the tears flow down your cheeks unbidden?" And then it advises, "Tell it to Jesus alone." There comes a time when you have to accept that there is no one but Jesus who you can tell that problem to. That's when words fail, tears flow, and your heart is so heavy, all you can do is turn it over to Jesus. If that's where you are right now, Jesus is waiting to comfort, heal your broken heart, and restore your faith in mankind. Don't walk around being damaged or depressed. That's not God's will for your life. Tell it to Jesus. And have a peace-filled day.

> *God is our refuge and strength, a very present help in trouble. (Psalm 46:1)*

> *Cast thy burden upon the LORD, and he shall sustain thee: he shall never suffer the righteous to be moved. (Psalm 55:22)*

What is that one thing which you cannot share with your friends nor family.

_____

_____

_____

_____

Today is the day to tell Jesus all about that sorrow. He will meet you where you are and lift that burden. Let Him.

Write what you need to share on a piece of paper. When you are ready to tell it to Jesus, read that script if you need to. Then, believe that it has been taken of. Destroy the paper as evidence that the problem has been destroyed. Then allow God's peace to fill you.

Constantly reminiscing will not get you too far ahead. Each time you stop your forward journey for a backward look, you delay the potential for a positive future. Moving forward says that you are no longer bound to, or controlled by, the things of your past. It means that you realize that better is on, and the only way to reach better is to go towards better. The Apostle Paul was so determined to press forward to his targeted goal, he declared that he would intentionally forget the things that are behind. That's what you need to do. Be intentional about your forward push, and leave the past alone. Free yourself for your higher calling. And have a determined day.

> *Brethren, I count not myself to have apprehended: but this one thing I do, forgetting those things which are behind, and reaching forth unto those things which are before, I press toward the mark for the prize of the high calling of God in Christ Jesus. (Philippians 3:13, 14)*

Today, be intentional in your desire to leave the past behind. Do not go back to the same conversation, behavior, or person. Press toward what you need, not what you had.

Who are you hiding from? Who has you so on the defensive that you can't even face yourself anymore? What have you done that is so horrible you can no longer face society? And where are you hiding? In your home, in the job, in the church? There is nothing hidden that will not be revealed, and no secret desire that will not be brought to light. So, stop hiding from man when God sees all. Instead, realize that you can hide in the arms of God. Though mother and father forsake you, as a hen gathers her children, so the Lord will hide you under His wings. So just trust in His security. And have a protected day.

> *For nothing is secret, that shall not be made manifest; neither any thing hid, that shall not be known and come abroad. (Luke 8:17)*

> *When my father and my mother forsake me, then the LORD will take me up. (Psalm 27:10)*

What are you running from?

_____
_____
_____
_____

What would be the positive result if today, you stopped and faced that "thing"?

_____
_____
_____
_____

Remember, "God has not given you a spirit of fear. Boldly face your fear and free yourself to live.

A word to the wise. Before you lock your doors and windows, make sure that the enemy is on the outside. There are times you feel secure because you have checked that you locked things down, only to realize that the enemy is within. In other words, don't look at others as the ones who hold you back or tie you down. And don't blame them when things don't work out right. Look within yourself and see what's hindering you from reaching your security. Remember, it's not the man who can destroy the body that you have to worry about. However, if you are sabotaging your own safety, the enemy is already inside. So, check yourself. And have a secure day.

> *For he that soweth to his flesh shall of the flesh reap corruption; but he that soweth to the Spirit shall of the Spirit reap life everlasting. (Galatians 5:8)*

Be honest with yourself. How and why are you hindering or sabotaging your own growth, success, health, relationships, or spiritual walk?

_____
_____
_____
_____

Choose the most important one and begin working to change that behavior and result. Then work on the next one as you begin to see change in the previous area.

Do you go through the daily ritual of fixing your hair in the mirror? You primp, or pull, you curl or tease? Or, if you don't have enough to play with, you slick it down or pick it out? Or maybe you have no hair at all, so you just check to be sure that a shave isn't needed? Then you leave the house, and immediately forget how your hair/head looks? Is that the way with your spiritual life? The scripture likens this to one who hears the word but does not the word. This means that you have to make sure that you look intently at the will of God, and abide in it. You can't forget what He expects of you, just as you can't forget that others are watching you. While you may forget what you saw in the mirror, there are those who will call you on what they see. So, check your spiritual mirror carefully and be sure that everything in you is in place. And have a self-awareness day.

> *For if any be a hearer of the word, and not a doer, he is like unto a man beholding his natural face in a glass: For he beholdeth himself, and goeth his way, and straightway forgetteth what manner of man he was. (James 1:23)*

What are you looking for when you look into the spiritual mirror?
___
___
___

What do you see?
___
___
___

Are you happy with the results? Why or why not?
___
___
___
___

If you need to, adjust what needs to be adjusted. Fix what's in need of repair. Be sure that what others see in you is truly what is in you.

Rest assured that what is for you, is for you. What has been promised will be fulfilled, and what has been ordained shall come to pass. However, whatsoever you sow, that too will be returned to you. The scripture says that it is yours to reap. So be careful what you sow. While you may be promised happiness, you will also reap the pain of the hurt that you sowed. While you are ordained for a life of prosperity, you will also reap the loss that you cause others to endure. So, remember, what is for you, it is for you, whether it be good or bad, so be careful what you plant. Sow responsibly. And have a bountiful day.

> *Be not deceived; God is not mocked: for whatsoever a man soweth, that shall he also reap. For he that soweth to his flesh shall of the flesh reap corruption; but he that soweth to the Spirit shall of the Spirit reap life everlasting. And let us not be weary in well doing: for in due season we shall reap, if we faint not. (Galatians 6:7, 8, 9)*

What is something which you have sown that you fear reaping?

_____
_____
_____
_____

What do you need to do to avoid that harvest?

_____
_____
_____
_____

It's never too late to go back and replant. Today, say sorry if you need to. Clear the air on that misunderstanding. Set some person free from the accusation that was brought against them.

Replant your seed so that you are certain about what you will be reaping.

Today, before you act, think. Before you speak, think. Before you respond in anger, think. Do not be hasty to act, speak, nor respond in anger. The scripture states that a person who is hasty is worse than a fool. You will destroy bridges that took years to build, and overturn progress that took tears to accomplish. So, take a minute to think things through before you break the slender thread of the relationship you are in, or damage the spirit of the one who depends on you. Remember, while actions speak louder than words, words can never be unsaid. So slow down your comeback. And have a peace-filled day.

> *Wherefore, my beloved brethren, let every man be swift to hear, slow to speak, slow to wrath: For the wrath of man worketh not the righteousness of God. (James 1:19, 20)*

Today, count to ten before you react. Just as you need to think before you speak, so too you must think before you act. Being right does not guarantee Brownie points.

And remember, everything that you do or say must glorify God.

Don't forget. Power is in the words that you speak. You speak life or death, happiness or grief, positivity or negativity. Think carefully about the energy that you release today. If you are speaking over your children, your spouse, your family, or your friends, speak only that which will be able to lift them higher to God and closer to you. Speak life into the dying relationships. Speak happiness into the grieving spirit. Speak positivity into the rebelling nature. Let only good go out from you, so that only good is accounted to you. Speak life. And have a power-filled day.

> *Death and life are in the power of the tongue: and they that love it shall eat the fruit thereof. (Proverb 18:21)*

Today, speak the power that is in you to create good. Create the relationships and life that you desire. Speak things as if they already exist. Let your words bring glory to God and life to others.

Vision is very important. You need vision to see where you are headed and how to get there. You need vision to see where you have been and how to avoid going back. You need vision to see who should be on your journey with you and who should be left behind. Without a vision, you will perish. Your dreams and desires will not be realized. So, before you take that first step forward, check your vision. And have an insightful day.

> *Where there is no vision, the people perish: (Proverbs 29:18a)*

What is that one thing which you are not willing to "see" or accept?
___
___
___
___

Why?
___
___
___
___

Now that you have finally admitted to being "intentionally blind," see what has been your obstacle, see what must be done to overcome it, and take care of the situation. Stop closing your "eyes" to the truth.

Reality check: just because they wish you well, it doesn't mean that they wish you well. Just because they say they are happy for you, it doesn't mean that they are happy for you. Just because they say they love you, it doesn't mean that they really love you. It's not about what they say. It's about what they do when they are done saying. There are those who will be with you today, and leave you hanging tomorrow. And there are those who will kiss you today, and already received their thirty pieces of silver to betray you yesterday. Remember, it's better to put confidence in God, than in man. Man will change up on you, but God remains the same, yesterday, today, and forever. So, know your circle. And have an honest day.

> *It is better to trust in the LORD than to put confidence in man. (Psalm 118:8)*

> *Jesus Christ the same yesterday, and to day, and for ever. (Hebrews 13:8)*

Whom in your circle have you been wondering about? Why?

_____
_____
_____
_____

How can you address the issue without losing sight of the true vision of glorifying God? What is your plan?

_____
_____
_____
_____

Remember, it is better to lose the whole world than to lose your soul.

The truth of the matter is, no one wants to be the one left alone, abandoned, or rejected. No one wants to be the one "they" decided they didn't want. No one wants to be the one who didn't fit the requirements. But if they had never rejected you, you would never be free to be who you were meant to be. Just think, when even your mother and father forsake you, the Lord will pick you up, dust you off, wash you clean, change your outward and inner man, give you a song the angels cannot sing, and a new name that no one will know until you do. Isn't that worth being rejected? So, don't worry and pine away. Instead, be glad. And have a rejoicing and worshipful day.

> *When my father and my mother forsake me, then the LORD will take me up. (Psalm 27:10)*
>
> *He that hath an ear, let him hear what the Spirit saith unto the churches; To him that overcometh will I give to eat of the hidden manna, and will give him a white stone, and in the stone a new name written, which no man knoweth saving he that receiveth it. (Revelation 2:17)*
>
> *And they sung as it were a new song before the throne, and before the four beasts, and the elders: and no man could learn that song but the hundred and forty and four thousand, which were redeemed from the earth. (Revelation 14:3)*

Who has rejected, forsaken, or abandoned you?

_____
_____
_____
_____

How has this impacted your relationship with others and with God?

_____
_____
_____
_____

What has this rejection released you to freely do or be?
_____
_____
_____
_____

Stop stressing what God has allowed, and start allowing what God has purposed for you.

You say that God is able. You claim that He is your strong tower. You decree and declare that your lack is over. You prophesy that the future is bright. And you state that all things work together for good, to those who love the Lord. Yet with all this positivity, you are living in the negative? Stop quoting the scriptures and start living them. You walk by faith, not by sight. That means that it's time to step out on the promises you talk about. Stop saying walls will fall, and start shouting the walls down. Stop saying that giants still fall, and start throwing the power of God at those giants. Stop talking victory, and start living victory. Your mountain will only move when your mustard seed faith tells it to move. So, step up your faith game. And have a victorious day.

> *For verily I say unto you, If ye have faith as a grain of mustard seed, ye shall say unto this mountain, Remove hence to yonder place; and it shall remove; and nothing shall be impossible unto you. (Matthew 17:20)*

> *For we walk by faith, not by sight: (2 Corinthians 5:7)*

What is that mountain or giant that you are still fearfully avoiding?
_____
_____
_____
_____

How have you proven the power of God in your life before?
_____
_____
_____
_____

Stop doubting what God can do when you've already seen what He has done. Today, tell your mountain to move, your wall to fall, and your giant to flee. Remember, speak your desire as if it already exists.

Generation after generation, things just seem to keep repeating. Broken homes, broken hearts, broken dreams. Families are torn apart, and children are drifting. No one seems to be able to keep it together. Then someone says, "Generational curse," and you accept that? No. The ground was cursed for your sin, and Christ was cursed and hung on a tree, for your sin. But by the sacrifice on the tree, your curse was lifted. Stop accepting the "curse" from those who don't know Christ and accept the freedom from the Christ who breaks all curses. No one can bless who God has cursed, and no man can curse who God has blessed. So, leave the curses for those who want to see you bound. And have a blessed day.

> *Christ hath redeemed us from the curse of the law, being made a curse for us: for it is written, Cursed is every one that hangeth on a tree: (Galatians 3:13)*

Today, speak the prophetic over your children and their children. Speak against every "perceived curse" in you family. There is no weapon formed against you that has the power to stand against the power of God.

Command every thing in your lives to align with the purpose and will of God.

When you give a gift to someone, do you keep going back to see where he or she has it stored, or hidden? To you constantly remind her that you gave it to her, and you hope she's keeping it safe until you need it again? Do you ask him to remind you of what the gift was, how it looked, what it cost? Then why do you keep going back to Jesus for what you entrusted Him with? If you gave it all to Jesus, let Him keep it. You don't need to know what he did with your past, or where He cast your sins. You don't need to check if He really is taking care of your history. He has erased your mistakes and is offering you a clean slate. Just trust Him that what you have handed to Him, He is able to handle. And have a redeemed day.

> *For the which cause I also suffer these things: nevertheless I am not ashamed: for I know whom I have believed, and am persuaded that he is able to keep that which I have committed unto him against that day. (2 Timothy 1:12)*

What is that burden or care which you "gave" to Jesus, yet you keep returning to it?

_____

_____

_____

What is your hope or intent in going back?

_____

_____

_____

If you truly believe that God is able to handle anything, let Him.

Write and say a prayer of repentance, asking God to forgive you for not trusting His ability to handle your situation.

_____

_____

_____

Then, just believe that God has it under control. And let Him take care of it.

Do you only go to the doctor when you know you are really ill? Or to the accountant only when you are being audited? What about the mechanic only when the car has finally stopped running? Are your dental visits based only on that deep numbing pain or swollen jaw? What about your talks with your savior? Are those based only on an "I need you right now Lord" basis? Do you only call him up when it seems like your world is falling apart? Just as you need to continually monitor your health before you need the experts to step in and save the day, so you need to monitor your relationship with God. Don't wait until the enemy has trampled on you to call on your protection. And don't wait until you are about to hear "depart from me," before you check that your soul is secure. Just as the doctor might not be able to fit you in, the judge won't give you time to make it right while you're already standing in front of Him. So, act while you have time. And have a spiritually healthy day.

> *For he saith, I have heard thee in a time accepted, and in the day of salvation have I succoured thee: behold, now is the accepted time; behold, now is the day of salvation. (2 Corinthians 6:2)*

When was the last time that you checked in with God to see what needed fixing in your relationship?

_____

_____

Did you make any adjustments?

_____

What do you still need to work on?

_____

_____

When is your deadline?

_____

_____

Remember, don't wait until it's too late to do your spiritual self-check.

Repossession means that something is being reclaimed by the rightful owner. They previously owned it, and based on the terms of a loan or agreement that were not met, they came to take back what belongs to them. Every business has the right to reclaim what is theirs, even down to the electric company. Don't pay the bill, and they take the power back. Don't pay the car note and they tow it away. So why are you leaving what's rightfully yours in the enemy's hands? It's time to repossess from the enemy's camp that which has been stolen or borrowed. Don't lose your inheritance because of fear. Take back your peace of mind, your joy, your family, and your future. Go on. Claim your rights as a child of the King. And have a restoration day.

> *And the LORD turned the captivity of Job, when he prayed for his friends: also the LORD gave Job twice as much as he had before. (Job 42:10)*

What have you lost to the enemy that needs to be reclaimed?

_____
_____
_____

What do you need to do to take back what is yours?

_____
_____
_____
_____

Create a plan for repossession, This may (or should) include prayer, fasting, praise, or worship. Determine for how long and, what specific times you will affect your plan. Whatever it entails, it's time to reclaim what is rightfully yours.

_____
_____
_____
_____
_____

When you make the decision to leave your family home, or church, you have to count the cost. Does leaving mean that you will be living down the block, across town, in another state, or another country? Does it mean that you're going to be visiting often, or never again? When you leave, can you go home again? Don't rush off because you have been given an inheritance, or you think you're all grown, or you just want to show that you don't need anyone, any more. When the prodigal son left home, he burnt bridges behind him, and when he needed to return, his father had to create new bridges to make him feel welcome again. Be careful who you disrespect or anger when you think it's time to go. They may not be as willing to offer the fattest calf when you do need to go home again. And while the heavenly Father waits to welcome you back, He said he will not strive with you forever. So, if you must go, go in peace and in love. And have an agreeable day.

> *He will not always chide: neither will he keep his anger for ever. He hath not dealt with us after our sins; nor rewarded us according to our iniquities. (Psalms 103:9, 10)*

Have you truly counted the cost of the decisions you have made?

What do you stand to lose?

_____

_____

_____

_____

What do you stand to gain?

_____

_____

_____

_____

If your losses are much more than your gains, you might want to, or need to, reconsider. Remember, it's not too late to fix what was damaged by that decision.

Be advised; don't let you voice be louder than your praise. Don't let you story be more genuine than your worship. And, don't let your boasting be stronger than your faith. Don't be like Peter who trusted in the power of his sword and not in the power of Christ's Word. Don't be like the disciples who jumped onto Peter's plan and had none of their own. And don't be the one who though you are warned that you are stumbling, still proceed to stumble and fall. Align your worship and your faith with the Word of God, so that when you are called to give an account of your time spent with Christ, you won't fall flat on your faith. Stand firm. And have an anointed day.

> *Thy word is a lamp unto my feet, and a light unto my path. (Psalms 119:105)*
>
> *And the Lord said, Simon, Simon, behold, Satan hath desired to have you, that he may sift you as wheat: But I have prayed for thee, that thy faith fail not: (Luke 22:31, 32a)*

What is the measure of your faith and worship? Are you merely going along with the crowd, or are you truly in that place of worshipping in spirit and in truth? Are you merely looking for the applause, or can God count on you when things become difficult?

Today, ask God to give you the know-how to walk according to His will and in His power and not your own.

Sometimes you have to get to the place where you accept that your way isn't working. You realize that you keep running into the same wall, tripping over the same obstacle, or falling into the same hole, time after time. This is when you have to be honest with yourself. You need somebody bigger and greater than you to take the wheel. You just need Jesus to take control. When you reach this place in your life, you will find yourself saying "Lord, I'm sorry. Sorry for thinking I could do this by myself. Sorry for wanting what you didn't decree for me. Sorry for complaining when I couldn't have my way." Then the Lord will take over and fix it. But you must get out of His way, and let your self-sufficiency fall by the way. He will do it if you just let Him. So, place your will in His hands. And have a divinely directed day.

> *A man's heart deviseth his way: but the LORD directeth his steps. (Proverbs 16:9)*

The LORD of hosts hath sworn, saying, Surely as I have thought, so shall it come to pass; and as I have purposed, so shall it stand: Isaiah 14:24

Let today be a day of surrender. Whatever you have tried, it has failed. Get out of the way and allow God to take the wheel of your life.

Write a prayer of total surrender to God. Tell Him what you are releasing to Him. Trust that He will fix it for you.

_____
_____
_____
_____

It's not because you're a bad person. It's not because you are cursed. And it's not because you've been having it too good, that you're being tested. It's because you've been praising God and trying to worship in all sincerity. It's because you've been attempting to honor Him in spirit and in truth. Your testing is created to test the level of your faith, your praise, and your worship. Just be assured that in all of your testing, God will make a way of escape. Keep praising through the testing. Keep worshipping through the struggles. And, keep extending your faith in the midst of what seems impossible. God is in control. Be strong in the Lord. And have a stress-free day.

> *And the LORD said unto Satan, Hast thou considered my servant Job, that there is none like him in the earth, a perfect and an upright man, one that feareth God, and escheweth evil? (Job 1:8)*

> *There hath no temptation taken you but such as is common to man: but God is faithful, who will not suffer you to be tempted above that ye are able; but will with the temptation also make a way to escape, that ye may be able to bear it. (1 Corinthians 10:13)*

> *Finally, my brethren, be strong in the Lord, and in the power of his might. (Ephesians 6:10)*

Today, when you are tested, remember that it is just that; a test.

Don't cheat, don't skip any of the test, and don't give up before the time is done. Have a plan for how you will handle your test.

My plan for when I'm being tested: I will...

_____

_____

_____

_____

Begin by studying for the test. Read the Word of God, prayerfully. This will ensure that you will be approved for the test itself. Then trust that the master teacher knows what you can handle. He will not give you more than you can bear.

Sometimes you notice that you are lacking something. It could be material, physical, emotional, social, or spiritual. You look around to find what's missing. You go shopping, to the gym, to a therapist, out with friends, or to church. You search and search, only to find that at the end of your journey, you are still lacking. The problem is not with finding what's lacking, but it's about knowing what's lacking. It's not about looking outward to find satisfaction. It's about knowing who can provide all that you need inside. Everything outside of you requires that you give something to gain what you lack. Only Jesus freely offers all that you need internally to survive. Remember, it's not about what you think you are lacking. It's about what God knows you need to be filled with. So, stop randomly searching and let Him do the supplying. And have a spirit-filled day.

> Jesus answered and said unto her, Whosoever drinketh of this water shall thirst again: But whosoever drinketh of the water that I shall give him shall never thirst; but the water that I shall give him shall be in him a well of water springing up into everlasting life. (John 4:13, 14)

What are you lacking spiritually?

_____
_____
_____
_____

Who do you have in your life that can help direct and encourage you in your spiritual journey?

_____
_____
_____
_____

Find someone, a minister, friend, or family member in whom you recognize the light of Christ. Ask him or her to study and/or pray with you as you seek to grow closer to Christ.

Have you finally reached your last alternative? Are you on your last backup plan? Have you reached the point of no return? And are you at your breaking point? Have you finally reached the end of that proverbial rope, and you're not sure how long you can hang on, or if you even want to? Have you tried everything that you possibly can? Have you truly tried Jesus? If you have tried Him, then all of the extremes that you have reached is His way of saying, "Now trust me." Take Him at His word that He will be your God, and you can put your confidence in Him. Every end that you reach is one more beginning for Him to work things out in your life. So, when you finally get to the end of your rope, just let go, and trust Him to catch you. And have a faith filled day.

> *Trust in the LORD with all thine heart; and lean not unto thine own understanding. In all thy ways acknowledge him, and he shall direct thy paths. (Proverbs 3:5, 6)*

What is, or what would be, your breaking point? If you've finally arrived there, what does it entail?

_____

_____

_____

_____

Pause for a moment in your panic, and hear the voice of Jesus saying, "I will never leave you nor forsake you." Know that He always keeps His word. Now let go of that "rope" and trust Him to catch you.

If you are wondering why you are wandering, stop for a minute and look around. Where are you? Do you know where you are headed? Do you even know how to get there? Are you planning on returning that way again? What about if you are not? Do you have a plan in mind for how you aim to progress beyond where you are now? If you are simply waiting for the Lord to direct your steps, but you have no idea where you want to go in Him, or if you even want to go in Him or with Him, you'll stay on the same spot. Stop wandering aimlessly along when the Lord has already revealed to you that you're headed in the wrong direction. That's why you're lost. He told you to launch out, but you are just sitting in the shallows for small fry to nibble, when He has the large fish for you to catch. Just follow His leading, and push and go forward. And have a God directed day.

> *Now when he had left speaking, he said unto Simon, Launch out into the deep, and let down your nets for a draught. And Simon answering said unto him, Master, we have toiled all the night, and have taken nothing: nevertheless at thy word I will let down the net. And when they had this done, they inclosed a great multitude of fishes: and their net brake. (Luke 5:4, 5, 6)*

Revisit your plan for where you want to go, whether in your career, relationship, or in Christ. Has God already told you "No"? Then it's time for a re-calibration. You may have lost your focus, but it's not too late to turn around. He has better for you, so it's time for you to stop stalling and get moving again. Refocus.

Write your new goal and plan below.

_____
_____
_____
_____

Start working on the first step of that plan.

Saying you love someone, but never showing you love that person, is the same as not saying it. So why say it? Love is something that is done, not merely said. Saying you want to be with someone, but looking at all the other someones, is as bad as cheating on that person. Similarly, saying you love Jesus while your heart is on the things of the world is not the same as showing that you love Him. Actions speak louder than words. Just as spending time together, calling or texting each other, or doing things for each other is important, so is the time and attention you give to your relationship with God. Remember, love is an action word. Show it, don't just say it. And have a love filled day.

> *No man can serve two masters: for either he will hate the one, and love the other; or else he will hold to the one, and despise the other. Ye cannot serve God and mammon. (Matthew 6:24)*
>
> *Charity suffereth long, and is kind; charity envieth not; charity vaunteth not itself, is not puffed up, Doth not behave itself unseemly, seeketh not her own, is not easily provoked, thinketh no evil; Rejoiceth not in iniquity, but rejoiceth in the truth; Beareth all things, believeth all things, hopeth all things, endureth all things. (1 Corinthians 13:4, 5, 6, 7)*

What can you do today to show the world that you love Christ?

_____
_____
_____
_____

What will you do to show Christ that you love Him?

_____
_____
_____
_____

The responses should be different for the two questions above. What you show in your relationship in private should not be the same as in public.

Fear can cause you to make compromises that will cost you dearly. Fear of the unknown is the greatest fear that exists. It is the not knowing, not being sure, not being prepared, that leads you to do things that you should not do. And, fear of the unknown can cause you to doubt the things that you do already know. However, fearing the unknown is a failure to trust God, for He is the God of the unknown. He knows all, and He has already gone ahead of you and cleared a way. He has straightened the crooked paths, and He has brought the high mountains low. And by the time you reach the unknown, the way will be prepared for your smooth journey. So, stop fearing the unknown, learn to trust the God who is all-knowing. And have a fearless day.

> *Peace I leave with you, my peace I give unto you: not as the world giveth, give I unto you. Let not your heart be troubled, neither let it be afraid. (John 14:27)*
>
> *Take therefore no thought for the morrow: for the morrow shall take thought for the things of itself. Sufficient unto the day is the evil thereof. (Matthew 6:34)*

What is the one fear that you are still struggling with in reference to your future or that of your children?

_____

_____

_____

What have you compromised on in order to cover or control this fear?

_____

_____

_____

Take a break from your fear and tell the Lord what you need Him to do for you so that you can move on from the place that you are stuck in.

_____

_____

_____

Now let it go and move on as if there was never a fear to think on.

Do you ever just get tired. Tired of trying, pushing, climbing, hoping, to make it through? Do you ever just want to throw your hands in the air, and declare that you've had enough? Do you ever just want to say, "Lord if it is possible, let this cup pass"? Do you ever just want to sit down and not move? Just let everything and everyone go? Just because you serve God, it doesn't mean that you won't get tired. And it doesn't mean that you don't want to give up. But because you serve Him, you know that you can do all things through Him who strengthens you. Say as Jesus said, "Father, not my will, but thy will be done." As long as you are moving according to His will, He will not allow you to face more than you can bear. So, take a deep breath, and say, "according to your will Lord." Now, let Him take control. And have a care-free day.

> *And he went a little further, and fell on his face, and prayed, saying, O my Father, if it be possible, let this cup pass from me: nevertheless not as I will, but as thou wilt. (Matthew 26:39)*
>
> *I can do all things through Christ which strengtheneth me. (Philippians 4:13)*

What are you tired of doing or handling?

_____
_____
_____
_____

Is there a way to lighten your load?

_____
_____

Who can you designate to help you carry the burden?

_____
_____

If you are in the fight alone, and if you know that it will be worth it in the end, you need to ask the Lord for added strength. And trust His will for your life. He will not let you carry more than you can handle.

Listen here. You've been going around taking up things that don't belong to you? You keep putting things in your bag, your wallet, and even your pockets? There are things in your bags that aren't yours to lift. There are things in your carry-on that you aren't supposed to carry. And there are items in your wallet and pocket that are too unimportant for you to be messing with. Stop picking up what God has put down. That bag of lies they told on you, that past that is in your carry-on, and those memories and images of the mess you were, which you keep in your pocket and wallet? Put them back down where God put them. Stop picking up history and allow God to write you your own story. Remember, each thing you pick up is another thing that God has to take out of your hands, again. So just leave them where He left them. Free yourself of excess baggage. And have a weightless day.

> *That ye put off concerning the former conversation the old man, which is corrupt according to the deceitful lusts; And be renewed in the spirit of your mind; And that ye put on the new man, which after God is created in righteousness and true holiness. (Ephesians 4:22, 23, 24)*
>
> *Wherefore seeing we also are compassed about with so great a cloud of witnesses, let us lay aside every weight, and the sin which doth so easily beset us, and let us run with patience the race that is set before us. (Hebrews 12:1)*

What are some weights that you have willingly taken up?

1. _____
2. _____
3. _____
4. _____
5. _____

What are you willing to sacrifice to carry these weights?

_____
_____
_____
_____

If you are tired of these weights, it's time to put them back where they belong. Be willing to let them go, and let God fill you with his peace and joy. Just ask Him to lift the loads that you carry.

_____
_____
_____
_____
_____
_____

How many of you have a closet filled with things that you use consistently? And how many of you have a closet stuffed with things that you are just longing to use, but there's never a good time, or place, or fit? You are like the closet. There are things shut up inside of you that need to be taken out and used, just because. Just because you feel like it, just because the occasion matters to you, just because someone else would find pleasure in you showcasing what you have. Saul told Timothy to stir up the gift that was in him. If you have it, why not use it for the glory of the Lord? Whether it's new or has been locked in your closet a long time, waiting to be birthed or introduced to the world, it's time to bring it out. Today, dust it off, and bless someone. And have an influential day.

> *Wherefore I put thee in remembrance that thou stir up the gift of God, which is in thee by the putting on of my hands. (2 Timothy 1:6)*

What is your hidden talent that the world is in need of?

_____

_____

_____

_____

What are you doing to cultivate this talent?

_____

_____

_____

_____

Who do you know that is in in need of what you have to offer?

_____

_____

_____

_____

Begin to share your gift with others and bless someone today.

Sometimes you think things are finally working out. You're smiling again. You have a song in your heart. Your footsteps are lighter. You even start looking forward to each day with anticipation. Then suddenly, you realize, it was too good to be true. It wasn't your song that was being played after all. It wasn't your accomplishment that was being applauded. And that drumroll you were hearing? It was just the thunderstorms beginning to crash in your life once more. But don't give up hope. For every storm there is a rainbow. And God is saying, "Never again will you walk in defeat. You may have to fight, and you may stumble, but never again will you lose." His covenant is sealed with the blood of His son. He is writing you a new song, and even the angels will rejoice at your comeback. So, smil, and get ready to take a bow. And have a break-through day.

> *These things I have spoken unto you, that in me ye might have peace. In the world ye shall have tribulation: but be of good cheer; I have overcome the world. (John 16:33)*
>
> *For whatsoever is born of God overcometh the world: and this is the victory that overcometh the world, even our faith. (1 John 5:4)*

When was the last time you felt as if things were actually going in your favor, but they were not?

_____

_____

_____

How did you feel? How did you react?

_____

_____

_____

Today, begin to praise God for your breakthrough. Don't wait for something to happen. Let your praise be the evidence of what is about to happen. God inhabits your praises, so He will show up when you begin to praise.

How many buildings do you pass each day that are decaying? The beauty is lost. The walls are broken, crumbling, or just gone. No faces look out of the windows. You question, who lived there, who are the owners that left it to decay, or, why is no one coming to restore it to its former beauty? Imagine one day, passing by and seeing a sign, "under construction." You wait with anticipation to see the finished product, and you hope it will be better than before. Is this the story of your life? Are there things that are broken, crumbling, or just plain gone? Don't worry. You too are carrying a sign that says, "under construction." As long as there's something of life left in you, Christ can fix you up and restore you to your divine status in Him. He will beautify you with salvation. And no longer will persons wag their heads when they pass by you. Your latter glory will be greater than your former. So, just wait on the Lord for your comeback. And have a renewed day.

> *For the LORD taketh pleasure in his people: he will beautify the meek with salvation. (Psalm 149:4)*

> *The glory of this latter house shall be greater than of the former, saith the LORD of hosts: and in this place will I give peace, saith the LORD of hosts. (Haggai 2:9)*

What is the condition of your spiritual house? Are you in a state of decay? Is your faith crumbling? Are you in need of a spiritual makeover?

_____

_____

_____

_____

Give God all of the broken pieces of your life and ask Him to fix you as new. He is waiting to restore you to the glory you can have only in Him.

Tell Him what is broken and what exactly it is that you need Him to attend to. Then let Him have His way.

_____

_____

_____

_____

BIBLE BITES

Make today a day of prayer. You haven't talked with God sincerely, recently, except for reminding Him of what you need Him to do. You've been calling Him up once a year to remind Him of the annual blessing, once a month to make sure the rent or mortgage is covered, once a week to get strength to face the job, and once a day to be protected from evil. But have you talked with Him at all? Have you given Him the chance to tell you what He wants from you? Were His wishes important enough for you to provide a ready ear? Did you hear Him say that He misses you, your devotion time, your sincere worship, your commitment to the relationship? It's not too late to get the conversation going. Stop talking to God, and talk with Him. Listen to His purpose for your life. As it is written, "He that has an ear, let Him hear what the Spirit is saying." Remember, it's not a one-sided conversation. Pay attention to the voice of God. And have a receptive day.

> *Come now, and let us reason together, saith the LORD: though your sins be as scarlet, they shall be as white as snow; though they be red like crimson, they shall be as wool. (Isaiah 1:18)*

When did you last "talk with" God? What was the content of that conversation?

_____

_____

_____

_____

If you haven't done so recently, listen to what He is saying to you today. Spend some time studying the Word and pay attention to what the Spirit is saying to you?

Write three things that have been revealed through or during your studies.

1. _____
2. _____
3. _____

How will you apply these discoveries to improving your relationship with God?

The question is asked, "Can two walk together except they agree?" While it is important to know that you are in agreement, you also have to understand what you are agreeing to or with, and why. Are you blindly following the crowd? Are you just trying to please someone? Are you fully committed to the cause being proposed? Or are you the mastermind of the plan? What are you agreeing to? Don't agree to lose your freedom, your personality, nor your spirituality just to be a part of the crowd. You'll be the one left holding the bag when plans fall apart. Instead, let the mind of Christ also be in you. Agee with His plan for your life, and you can walk without fear or concern. Trust His will and guarantee. And have a guiltless day.

> *Finally, brethren, whatsoever things are true, whatsoever things are honest, whatsoever things are just, whatsoever things are pure, whatsoever things are lovely, whatsoever things are of good report; if there be any virtue, and if there be any praise, think on these things. (Philippians 4:8)*

What is something that you have recently agreed to, but you did not want to?

_____

_____

_____

Why did you agree? (Personal of professional reasons?)

_____

_____

_____

How will this bring honor or glory to God?

_____

_____

_____

Remember, it's never too late to change your mind to align it with God's plan for your life.

How do you measure your accomplishments? Is it by the money you make, the material possessions you own, the type of job that you do? Or have you righted any wrongs, dried someone's tears, calmed a trouble spirit? How do you measure your accomplishments? Have you left your name on a star, in lights, or in the Lamb's book of life? How do you measure your accomplishments? Have you led anyone to find himself, find her purpose, find hope in Christ? Accomplishments cannot be measured by what you were able to attain by yourself, but by what you are able to maintain through and for Christ. Remember, you can do all that you can, but only what's done for Christ will last. So, strive to make a future built on Christ. And have a fulfilling day.

> *Lay not up for yourselves treasures upon earth, where moth and rust doth corrupt, and where thieves break through and steal: But lay up for yourselves treasures in heaven, where neither moth nor rust doth corrupt, and where thieves do not break through nor steal: For where your treasure is, there will your heart be also. (Matthew 6:19, 20, 21)*

What do you consider to be your greatest accomplishment? Why?

_____

_____

_____

_____

Will this accomplishment make you happy five years in the future? Ten years? Why or why not?

_____

_____

_____

_____

Will it benefit anyone other than yourself?

If you still feel unfulfilled after reviewing your accomplishment, try inspiring someone to be a better version of himself or herself.

Do you have a friend, a real friend, a best friend? Do you have someone you can talk to, turn to, be real to? Can you trust him, confide in him, and depend on him? Can you call him up at any time, anywhere, in any situation? Do you have a friend who loves you in spite of your flaws, and because of your flaws? Is this friend understanding of the mistakes you make, does he forgive them, and help you avoid them? If you don't have such a friend, when you find him, hold on to him. Treasure him, shower him with appreciation, and love him like a brother. You can find this friend in Jesus. When you meet Him, He will say, "I call you no more servants, but friends." He loves you, looks out for you, and defends you. And, He understands your mistakes, sees your flaws, and loves you in spite of it all. So, there's no need to go this journey alone. Just accept the hand of friendship and love that Christ is offering. Lean on Him. And have an amiable day.

> *A man that hath friends must shew himself friendly: and there is a friend that sticketh closer than a brother. (Proverbs 18:24)*

> *Henceforth I call you not servants; for the servant knoweth not what his lord doeth: but I have called you friends; for all things that I have heard of my Father I have made known unto you. (John 15:15)*

Reread the qualifications above. List at least three friends who meet these qualifications.

1. _____
2. _____
3. _____

As soon as possible, let these friends know that you appreciate them, and why.

Now, write a note to Jesus letting Him know how much you appreciate Him. Be sure to tell Him also.

_____
_____
_____

What is your heart's desire? What do you want more than anything? Do you long for money, fame, position, authority, unlimited power? Do you want to be healthy, happy, independent, free from all cares? What do you want more than anything? Do you want supernatural strength, the ability to see the invisible, to be able to move at the speed of light? What do you want more than anything? Do you want boldness like Peter, faith like Abraham, courage like David? Or is it enough to be like Paul, to simply "know Him"? Or like Zacchaeus, to simply "see Him"? Maybe you are like the woman with the issue of blood, and you just want "to touch Him." Whatever your desire is, let it be to the honor and glory of God. In all your ways acknowledge Him, and he will make you to walk in paths that you never wanted to, or thought you could, walk on. Whatever it is that you want more than anything, seek Christ first, and all things will be added unto you. Prove Him. And have a rewarding day.

> *But seek ye first the kingdom of God, and his righteousness; and all these things shall be added unto you. (Matthew 6:33)*

What is your heart's desire?

_____

_____

_____

_____

How does it fit in with God's will for your life?

_____

_____

_____

_____

Remember to seek God's will as you go after the thing that you desire most. Let it be to His honor and glory.

Your mind can be your greatest asset, but it can also be your greatest enemy. What you focus on is what you internalize, what you believe, and what you become. So, stop focusing on the things that cause you to doubt. Stop believing that you're less than what you are. Stop setting yourself up to become what they said you would become. Believe that you have overcome the world, you are a victor, and you are redeemed. Whatsoever things are lovely, whatsoever things are true, whatsoever things are of good report, think on those things. Let what God thinks for you become what you think for yourself. And have a clarifying day.

> Finally, brethren, whatsoever things are true, whatsoever things are honest, whatsoever things are just, whatsoever things are pure, whatsoever things are lovely, whatsoever things are of good report; if there be any virtue, and if there be any praise, think on these things. (Philippians 4:8)

What are some negative thoughts that have been overpowering your mind lately?

___

___

___

What is at the roots of these thoughts?

___

___

___

When you have examined where these thoughts are originating, intentionally begin to rewrite these thoughts. (For example; "You will never make it" becomes, "I can do all things through Christ.") Repeat this for each negative thought that surfaces.

Negative thought:

___

___

Rewritten thought:

___

___

If you are still trying to impress others, you are wasting your time. You can't impress those who don't know what a real blessing looks like. They'll look at every blessing you receive and call it luck. They'll look at every victory you gain and call it coincidence. They'll look at every breakthrough and call it accidental. Stop trying to make persons appreciate you or be happy for you. By the time they realize what you have been blessed with, they'll also realize what they have missed. And remember, although you are blessed to bless others, not everyone you know is to be a recipient of your blessing. Sometimes the blessing is for you alone. So just let them remain unimpressed, while you remain totally blessed. And have a divinely favored day

> *Therefore God give thee of the dew of heaven, and the fatness of the earth, and plenty of corn and wine: Let people serve thee, and nations bow down to thee: be lord over thy brethren, and let thy mother's sons bow down to thee: cursed be every one that curseth thee, and blessed be he that blesseth thee. And Esau said unto his father, Hast thou but one blessing, my father? bless me, even me also, O my father. And Esau lifted up his voice, and wept. Genesis (27:28, 29, 38)*

Who are you trying to impress, and why?

Name:
_____

Reason:
_____
_____

Name:
_____
_____

Reason:
_____
_____

Are you required to be accountable to any of the above persons?

No.

Yes.

If your answer is "No", then, stop trying to impress others. Just live a life that is pleasing to God. All things will fall into place if you just live for Christ. He is the only one you need to be approved by.

If your answer is "Yes," just do what is required of you. Your honest work and service is all that's needed. That is required by God.

When you are facing a battle, in a battle, or thinking of starting a battle, think reinforcements. Think of what you need to protect you, sustain you, and strengthen you. Think of the weapons that will be formed against you. Think of the fiery darts of the enemy that will be launched in your direction. Think of the wicked who will come against you to eat you up. Then think of reinforcements. Think of the whole armor of God to keep you protected. Think of the angels of the Lord that will encamp round about you to fend off the darts. Think of the Holy Spirit dwelling inside of you to keep you sustained. Knowing that you are inside of the name of the Lord, and that He is your strong tower, what will you fear? Knowing who fights your battles, who commands the angelic hosts, and who is in agreement with the Holy Spirit, you have all the reinforcement you need. So be strong in the Lord, secure your armor, stand like true soldiers of God. And have a fortified day.

> *Put on the whole armour of God, that ye may be able to stand against the wiles of the devil. For we wrestle not against flesh and blood, but against principalities, against powers, against the rulers of the darkness of this world, against spiritual wickedness in high places. Wherefore take unto you the whole armour of God, that ye may be able to withstand in the evil day, and having done all, to stand. (Ephesians 6:11, 12, 13)*

What battle will you fight today?

_____
_____
_____
_____

What part of the "Armor of God" are you lacking or missing for your battle?

_____
_____
_____
_____

What are you doing to get the reinforcements you will need to have on hand?
_____
_____
_____
_____

Remember, without your armor, you are merely a target.

To be satisfied means that you are content with the way things are. It means that you are at peace with the way things are and have no complaints. But there are times when you have no reason to complain and yet you make reasons. Then you wonder why things aren't going as they once did. Here's why. The bible states that it's better to live in a corner of the housetop, than in a wide house with a brawling woman. Stop finding reasons to sow discord and start appreciating what you have. Remember, better is little with the fear of the LORD than great treasure with turmoil. If you are satisfied with the little God has given, only then can He trust you with much. It makes no sense to complain yourself out of your happiness or your blessing. So, learn to be content and watch God honor your meekness. And have a rewarded day.

> *Better is little with the fear of the LORD than great treasure and trouble therewith. (Proverbs 15:16)*
>
> *It is better to dwell in a corner of the housetop, than with a brawling woman in a wide house. (Proverbs 21:9)*

What is your major complaint today?

_____
_____
_____
_____

What are two things that you can do to stop the need to complain?

1. _____
   _____

2. _____
   _____

Unless your complaining is garnering results, why complain? Fix what can be fixed and find someone who can fix what you can't.

No matter how many times you fall down, how many times you are pushed down, how many times you are kept down, get back up again. Don't let anyone see you down and count you out. Even if the count goes to nine, you have to get up before they count you out. When Jesus refused the woman whose daughter was ill, she was willing to receive the crumbs. If you are willing to take even the crumbs, you have to get up to gather them. They may want you to give up, but just as the woman with the issue of blood kept going until she touched her intended target, so must you. Even while you feel yourself slipping, tell yourself, "I'll get back up again." So, as hard as it may be, it's time to get up and push on. And have a resilient day.

> *The steps of a good man are ordered by the LORD: and he delighteth in his way. Though he fall, he shall not be utterly cast down: for the LORD upholdeth him with his hand. (Psalms 37:23, 24)*
>
> *Fear thou not; for I am with thee: be not dismayed; for I am thy God: I will strengthen thee; yea, I will help thee; yea, I will uphold thee with the right hand of my righteousness. (Isaiah 41:10)*

Today, tell yourself you are not staying down. Get up, dust off your emotional self, and get back in the game.

When the day is over, write a review of the victorious day you had, just because you refused to stay down.

_____
_____
_____
_____

Do you have a testimony of what the Lord has done for you? Can you tell of His goodness, His, mercy, or His grace? Do you have the evidence of things not seen, the manifestation of things asked for, proof beyond comprehension that He is a miracle working God? Have you tried Him and found Him to be all that He promised? If God has brought you out, taken you through, and made a way where there was clearly no way, now is the time to declare that He is God, and there is none like Him. When you tell your story, He receives the glory. And that's what it's all about. So, tell someone about the good news, of God's favor, and show them that He can do the same for them. Lift Him up to others and He will lift you up in due season. Go ahead, big Him up. And have a celebration day.

> *I have preached righteousness in the great congregation: lo, I have not refrained my lips, O LORD, thou knowest. I have not hid thy righteousness within my heart; I have declared thy faithfulness and thy salvation: I have not concealed thy lovingkindness and thy truth from the great congregation. (Psalms 40:9, 10)*

What is the testimony which you can share with someone today to encourage him or her in the struggle?

_____

_____

_____

_____

Let someone know that with God, nothing is impossible.

When was the last time you paid attention to the potholes on your roads? Try this. As you come to each hole, see it as the test and trial you must face to make it through. Sometimes a bump sends you upward and you feel as if you're not going to have an easy landing. But, you eventually come down, and keep right on going. Other times, when you hit a hole, you feel the dip that leaves you uneasy or queasy. You think you're going to be sick. But, a few minutes later, that has passed, and the hole is merely a memory. When you face your testing and trials, tell yourself, "I do not know if it will be an easy landing, or if I'll feel fit to carry on, but that too shall pass." If you could avoid every bump, you wouldn't need a mechanic, just as if you could avoid every trial or test, you wouldn't need Jesus. But you do. So just fasten your seat belt and face every bump with the assurance that this too shall pass. Just trust the master driver. And have a secure day.

> *Yea, though I walk through the valley of the shadow of death, I will fear no evil: for thou art with me; thy rod and thy staff they comfort me. (Psalms 23:4)*

What is the condition of the spiritual road that you are traveling?

_____
_____
_____
_____

Are you feeling uneasy or scared about the journey? Why?

_____
_____
_____
_____

Find and internalize scriptures which reassure you of God's presence. He will never leave you nor forsake you. Just trust Him.

_____
_____
_____
_____

As you are spring cleaning, remember to sort your things before you toss them away. Be careful with "important" documents. Some things you will want to keep, but they need to go. Just because they have sentimental value, that's not the right reason to hold on to them. Let them go. And there are some that you have several copies of, but you only need one. Let the others go. Just as when God is ready to clean some things and people out of your life, and you want to hang on to them for sentimental reasons. Some of them you don't need at all, and some of them you have too many of. Let them go. Then, there are clothes which no longer fit you, or represent you, but you still want to wear them? Let them go. Just as when some behaviors, attitudes, and postures no longer fit you as a child of God, and you have to let them go. God is ready to bring some new into your life, but He needs room to do so. So, allow Him to declutter and transform your old. And have a renewed day.

> *And be not conformed to this world: but be ye transformed by the renewing of your mind, that ye may prove what is that good, and acceptable, and perfect, will of God. (Romans 12:2)*
>
> *Remember ye not the former things, neither consider the things of old. (Isaiah 43:18)*

Find three material items which represent behaviors, attitudes, and persons in your life which you have outgrown. You will be discarding them. Write the item and what it represents on the lines below. When you have released an item, follow through with letting go of the person or attitude it represents.

Item 1.
_____

Item 2.
_____

Item 3.
_____

When you have released the things that you no longer need, fill the empty space with the Word of God, with psalms, and praise. Let God bring in the new that He has for you.

When was the last time you turned your phone off? Not because you were on a plane, or the battery was drained, or you were trying to avoid someone. But just because. Just because you wanted some time to think, to focus on God, to communicate with Him without interruption? Just because you wanted to call Him up, and you didn't want any dropped calls? Sometimes you have to turn off some modes of communication just to hear what God is saying. People will keep calling and interrupting your conversation with Him unless you make His call a priority. So just for one day, turn off all other voices except for the voice of God. Really talk to Him, talk with Him, listen to Him, and really begin to understand what He's been trying to tell you ever since you lost contact with Him. He's feeling neglected and rejected. But, He still wants to hear from you, because He loves you. So today, turn off the outward distractions, tune in to Jesus. And have a spiritually filled day.

> *Shew me thy ways, O LORD; teach me thy paths. Lead me in thy truth, and teach me: for thou art the God of my salvation; on thee do I wait all the day. (Psalms 25:4, 5)*

Go without your phone today. Instead of talking to friends, texting, or scrolling social media sites, use that time to read a book, study the scriptures, write a love letter to God.

Dear God:

_____

_____

_____

_____

At the end of the day, use your phone to post about the awesome day that you spent in the presence of the Lord.

There's someone you are waiting on for a sorry. You've been waiting for a very long time, imagining just how free you will feel when you finally hear it. You've thought of the burden that will be lifted from your shoulders. You have anticipated the moment when you can move on with your life. But what if it never happens? What if that someone chooses not to say sorry? Are you going to stay bound and limited, waiting on a sorry? The scripture advises us to simply forgive. It doesn't say to wait for someone to apologize. It says to forgive. In forgiving others, you have to accept that they may not be sorry, and you have to be sorry. Sorry that you wanted more than they are able to give. Sorry that they never knew how much they mattered. Sorry that you didn't matter as much to them as you thought. Then forgive yourself for holding on to the hurt and loss, and move on. Time is too short to spend it on unforgiving. So, set yourself free; forgive. And have a grace filled day.

> *Therefore if thou bring thy gift to the altar, and there rememberest that thy brother hath ought against thee; Leave there thy gift before the altar, and go thy way; first be reconciled to thy brother, and then come and offer thy gift. (Matthew 5:23, 24)*

> *And when ye stand praying, forgive, if ye have ought against any: that your Father also which is in heaven may forgive you your trespasses. But if ye do not forgive, neither will your Father which is in heaven forgive your trespasses. (Mark 11:25, 26)*

Who are you waiting on for a sorry?
_____
_____

What will you have to give up if you do not receive that sorry?
_____
_____

What will you truly gain when/if you get that sorry?
_____
_____

Is there someone who you need to say sorry to? Go ahead and do it. Set yourself free, and set the other person/s free also. If you don't receive a sorry, at least you've made things right with God.

So, you've been in a struggle. It has been long and hard. You were at times on top, but most often you were at the bottom. Now, it's over. You look in the mirror and what do you see? Just cuts and bruises that tell the story of your struggle. Yes, you've been bruised, but not broken. You've been cut, but not crushed. You've been dragged about, but not defeated. Each mark you see says that you were a victim, but you're victorious. You've been tried, but you've triumphed. Don't even try to cover the cuts and bruises. When people talk about you, and they will, let them talk of how you went to the wall, and walked away a winner. They're going to use your testimony to tell others that when they are tested, and tried, and even trampled on, they can still get up, and walk away. And when the next struggle comes, as it will, remember, that scar you carry from the last battle is proof that you got over. So, face the struggles as a true soldier. And have a conquering day.

> *And not only so, but we glory in tribulations also: knowing that tribulation worketh patience; And patience, experience; and experience, hope: And hope maketh not ashamed; because the love of God is shed abroad in our hearts by the Holy Ghost which is given unto us. (Romans 5:3, 4, 5)*

Reflect on each scar that you have, and detail the turning point of the battle. Focus on the place where you realized that you were going to walk away a victor.

_____

_____

_____

_____

Now, stop stressing over the scars that you see from the battles you've won. Victims aren't left to tell their story.

Remind yourself that you are a winner. Then walk with your head high like a winner should.

Are you someone who is stuck in a bad relationship or situation? Do you wonder why you stay, or keep going back for more? Do you question if you really want to be free? Do you even know that you can be free? What if you were given other options? Would you choose to go back to the old and familiar? Why? Don't get comfortable being chained. It's really not about the freedom. It's about the value of the freedom. So, do you know the value of being free? Do you know the price that was paid for your freedom? Do you know the blood that was shed for your liberty? If you've never been free, you'll be content to be chained. But if you were once free, you will fight to remain so. Don't remain bound out of familiarity. At some point you will have to say, "Okay God, I'm ready to be free." And if you allow Him to, He will get you out and keep you out. Remember, he who the Son sets free is free indeed. Don't settle for chains when you can wear a crown. Walk free. And have a liberated day.

> *If the Son therefore shall make you free, ye shall be free indeed. (John 8:36)*

What or whom do you need to be loosed from?
_____
_____

Why have you stayed in this situation?
_____
_____

What is your role in the difficulties?
_____
_____

If you have truly tried but have been unable to "escape" the problem, it's time to tell God that you are ready to be free.

You have to be clear about what you want and when you want it. Trust God to take of it, and be prepared to move when He sets you free.

Tell God exactly what you need Him to do for you to be free.
_____
_____
_____

Have you ever been told a real bold-faced, intentional lie? Did the liar look you directly in the eyes and clearly pronounce every word? Was he so convincing that you believed him, even just for a minute? Were you so taken in by the skill of the liar that you still doubt if it was a lie or the truth? Has anyone ever told you the truth? A real heartwarming, honest-to-goodness truth? Did she look you in the eyes? Did she clearly pronounce every word? Did she sound so convincing that you could never doubt what was said, but yet, you can't believe that truth? Now how do you know the lie from the truth if they both look alike? Some people speak both lies and truth, so It's up to you to know the difference. Remember, the truth will set you free. But, if after its said, you are still lost, wondering, or afraid, it's not truth. Truth is intended to deliver, not depress. So, know the difference. Seek the truth at all cost, pray to discern the lies. And have an honest day.

And ye shall know the truth, and the truth shall make you free. (John 8:32)

Try asking each person you interact with today to be totally honest with you. Ask what you really want to know and be prepared for the responses'

Write three questions that you will ask.

1. _____
_____
2. _____
_____
3. _____
_____

How do you know if the responses you received were truly honest answers?
_____
_____

Ask God for discernment to know a lie from the truth.
_____
_____

In the midst of your down moments, when you feel alone, and not sure why, that's the time God is getting ready to do something new. You sit and worry or wonder. You question and agonize over the details. You toss options around in your mind and still have no idea what to do. That's the time to let go and let God do something new. Suddenly you realize that there is nothing in your life which God cannot handle. You realize that if you trust Him, He will come through for you. You accept that you can do all things through Christ who strengthens you. That's the time that God did something new. Each time the enemy brings doubts or fears to shake your confidence in God, that's when he knows that God is about to send the new. He's trying to get you to expect less, ask for less, and receive less. But if you just trust in the power of God, the enemy will find out that God only operates in the new. So, face those down moments in preparation for the up. And have a renewed day.

> *Have not I commanded thee? Be strong and of a good courage; be not afraid, neither be thou dismayed: for the LORD thy God is with thee whithersoever thou goest. (Joshua 1:9)*

What is the new thing that God has been moving you toward, but you have been pushing back against?

_____
_____

_____

Stop delaying your blessing.

Today, when that idea presents itself, or that door of opportunity opens up, step through.

Record the experience below.

_____
_____
_____
_____
_____

You have had friends for years who yet know nothing about you. They've been there through your school days, college, and marriage, got into trouble with you, or got you into trouble. They laughed with you and cried with you. Yet they don't know the secret details of your past life. But don't you wish there was someone in your life who knew all the negative about you, yet came to find you when it mattered most, who showed up just at the right time? Like the woman at the well of Samaria, you always need someone who shows up on time, knows all of your secrets, and uses the dark past of your life to show you a better future. With five men, you'd think there would have been at least one who could have offered her hope. But when even those who "know" you can't help, Jesus will show up at your well. He will know about the mess in your life and change it into a message, so that you can help others find Him. So, don't despair. Meet Him at your well. And have a refreshing day.

> *Come, see a man, which told me all things that ever I did: is not this the Christ? And many of the Samaritans of that city believed on him for the saying of the woman, which testified, He told me all that ever I did. (John 4:29, 39)*

What is some dark thing from your past that not even your closest friend knows about?

_____
_____
_____

Why are you afraid to share this information?

_____
_____
_____

How can you use that thing to share the message of God's love?

_____
_____
_____

Go ahead and share your experience. Someone needs to know that God forgives anything.

Love is supposed to be a beautiful thing. It makes the world go around, covers a multitude of evil, and is not selfish. Love thinks of others before self. Love changes people, and the list goes on. But in spite of all that love can do, there is still so much ugliness in the world. People you love don't love you back. Lovers cheat, lie, and selfishly demand more love. Then they claim that they love you. So, what can you do? Understand, it's not really about those who don't know what it means to love. It's about you who have experienced real love; the love of God, the sacrifice of His Son, and the gift of eternal life. When you think of the times you've been selfish, lied to God, cheated on Him, and yet He still loved you. How can you not still love? "Love suffers long, and is kind." However, remember, with Jesus, there comes a time when He will no longer wait for you to change, to love Him unconditionally. So, love wisely, love honestly. And have a reciprocated day.

Charity suffereth long, and is kind; (1 Corinthians 13:4a)

Herein is love, not that we loved God, but that he loved us, and sent his Son to be the propitiation for our sins. Beloved, if God so loved us, we ought also to love one another. (1 John 4:10, 11)

Are you still waiting for someone to say I love you?

Find at least five scriptures which speaks about the love of God for you.

1. _____
2. _____
3. _____
4. _____
5. _____
6. _____

Use these scriptures to encourage yourself whenever you feel the need to be loved.

What does it mean to be confident? Is it having a spirit of boldness, or lacking fear? What does confidence look like? Is it shoulders pushed back, stomach stuck up, and head in the air? What does it take to be confident? Is it knowing that you're strong enough to hold your own in a fight, throw the first punch, look someone in the eye without flinching? None of this is confidence if you're shaking inside while acting brave on the outside. Confidence is being aware that you are heading toward a battle, but being secure in the knowledge that you won't have to fight it because the battle belongs to the Lord. It's knowing that in the midst of the storm, you need not fear because Christ is in the storm with you. Confidence is knowing that when the enemy sends weapons against you, they shall not prosper. In short, confidence is knowing who is in charge of the outcome of every situation that you encounter. So, stop acting brave and start living faith. And have a trusting day.

> *No weapon that is formed against thee shall prosper; and every tongue that shall rise against thee in judgment thou shalt condemn. This is the heritage of the servants of the LORD, and their righteousness is of me, saith the LORD. (Isaiah 5)4:17*

Have you been "putting on" an "act" of bravery?

Today is your day to start living by faith and not by fear.

Start declaring that you are "the head and not the tail." You are "a conqueror." You are "surrounded by the angels of the Lord." When you know who you are and whose you are, there is no need to tiptoe into battle. You are a child of the heavenly King.

Live your confidence.

What other scriptures can you add, which speak to your victory?

_____
_____
_____
_____

What is the difference between realization and revelation? With realization, you are working from a place of knowing without understanding. You knew the price you had to pay for your actions, but you didn't realize the long-term consequences involved. You knew it would be wrong to say what you said, but you didn't realize that it would come back to be a thorn and annoyance for years. But when you have revelation, you are dealing from a place of ignorance and newness. You were ignorant of the fact that you were lost without Christ. But when you found Him, a new life, nature, and creation was revealed. His mercy was revealed. His grace was revealed. His power was revealed. So, if what you are being told isn't bringing newness to your ignorance, it isn't revelation, it's realization. People realize your pain, but God reveals His healing power. So, trust in the newness of God's revealing power and not in the realization of the preacher or teacher. And have an awakened day.

> *Surely the Lord GOD will do nothing, but he revealeth his secret unto his servants the prophets. (Amos 3:7)*

> *For the prophecy came not in old time by the will of man: but holy men of God spake as they were moved by the Holy Ghost. (2 Peter 1:21)*

What are some realizations that you have experienced recently? How have they impacted your daily life?

_____
_____
_____
_____

What is something that God has revealed to you? How will you use this revelation to move to a deeper relationship with God?

_____
_____
_____
_____

When God reveals His will and purpose to you, realize that it is an opportunity for you to grow. Never take it for granted.

Do you ever think of what you eat? Some foods contain similar ingredients, serving the same purpose. Some make the skin soft or firm it up. Inside, some foods make you sick, harden you or heal you. And what goes inside you will be reflected on the outside. If you eat unhealthy foods, your skin will show it. If your arteries are hardened, it will eventually show up on the outside. So, it is with the Holy Spirit. You can have it on the outside or the inside. It will be the same ingredient, and it can work in any way. But what happens on the outside is much different from what happens when you have it on the inside. The Holy Spirit outside will surround you and protect you. But on the inside, it will fill, renew, strengthen and transform you. But you have to know the difference, because there's always a consequence or benefit to what goes inside. As what you eat is who you are, so what dwells in you is who you are. So, eat wisely, and spiritually. And have a wholesome day.

> *But the fruit of the Spirit is love, joy, peace, longsuffering, gentleness, goodness, faith, Meekness, temperance: against such there is no law. (Galatians 5:22, 23)*

What foods are you partaking of that are unhealthy?

_____
_____
_____
_____

What are you partaking of that is hindering your spiritual growth?

_____
_____
_____
_____

Today, pay attention to what you eat naturally and spiritually. Read the ingredients carefully. Say "No" to anything that will cause you negative consequences.

Do you understand the value of light? When you have it, you take it for granted. But when it's gone, you realize just how important it really is. You begin to notice just how dark blackness really can be. It is then you need the light to light your way, as you need the inner light to direct your path. You need to be able to see the traps that are set, and the doors that are open. You need to see when the danger is near, and when the blessing is passing your way. You need to see who is rooting for your downfall and who is really cheering you on. Without this inner light, you will enter a place of darkness, a place without hope, and without promise. So, when you do find yourself in the light, stay in it. When you find yourself outside of the light, draw near to it. Finally, you'll find the light inside of you, and it will radiate to all who live in the darkness. So just allow your life to be the light that God will use to guide others to him. And have a brilliant day.

> *This then is the message which we have heard of him, and declare unto you, that God is light, and in him is no darkness at all. (1 John 1:5)*
>
> *Let your light so shine before men, that they may see your good works, and glorify your Father which is in heaven. (Matthew 5:16)*

Are you or someone you know floundering around in darkness?

_____

If you are in a place of darkness, how do you plan on getting back to the light?

_____
_____
_____

What plan can you implement that will help someone else back to their light?

_____
_____
_____

Remember, staying in the dark is a choice.

It's been a long time coming. That song, that joy, that praise; it's been a long time coming. You've watched others be promoted over you, had some walk away and left you, and had friends and family despise your character. But you knew that day would come. You knew that you would sing again shout again, and praise again. It's been a long time coming, but it's coming. You've been crying, but it's coming. You've been broken, but it's coming. You've even been running, but it's coming. Stop running, stop crying, stop questioning. Just tell yourself, "My day of release is coming. My new beginning is coming. My victory is knocking." Your day is here. Open and receive what you've been waiting for, for so long. And have a rewarding day.

> *They that sow in tears shall reap in joy. He that goeth forth and weepeth, bearing precious seed, shall doubtless come again with rejoicing, bringing his sheaves with him. (Psalms 126:5, 6)*

What have you been patiently waiting for?
_____
_____
_____
_____

What have you lost in the time that you have been waiting?
_____
_____
_____
_____

Begin today to thank God for the breakthrough that is headed your way. Remember, you don't have to see it to claim it.

You've heard it said before, "If you are afraid of the heat, stay out of the kitchen." But how will you learn to cook? If you avoid the battle because of your fear of being scarred, you will never know the feeling that comes with winning. The trick to your victory isn't to avoid the heat, but to wear protection from the heat. Just as you wouldn't go to battle without your war gear, so you must be clothed for your spiritual battle with the whole armor of God. A true soldier does not run from the heat of the battle, he voluntarily enlists to serve. He prepares for the fight with the best means of protection. And he pays close attention to the directions of his Captain. So, when you are ready to cook, wear your mittens and protective apron, and when, you are ready to win the battle, put on the whole armor of God. And quit you like men, and be strong. Stop running from your training ground. Just step up to the challenge. And have a winning day.

> *Put on the whole armour of God, that ye may be able to stand against the wiles of the devil. (Ephesians 6:11)*
>
> *Watch ye, stand fast in the faith, quit you like men, be strong. (1 Corinthians 16:13)*

Have you enlisted in the spiritual army?
___

Do you follow the directions given by your captain? Why or why not?
___
___
___

Are you fully armored and prepared for the fight?
___
___

How can you ensure that you will be ready when the battle is called again?
___
___

If you are in the fight but you're not prepared to fight, you might want to reconsider your enlistment.

Although the scripture says to consider them, have you given much thought to the lilies of the field? Have you considered their beauty or the variety of colors and shades? God's majesty and power is reflected in the lilies. They do not worry nor work, nor seek to create beauty for themselves. They just are, because God wills them to be. What about the birds? They do not fly around stressing about the next meal, nor try to amass grain for tomorrow. They simply trust that each day, they shall be fed. Are you not more important than the flower or the bird? Were you not worth the gift of God's Son? Were you not worth His blood being shed? Do you not trust Him that He shall supply all your needs, according to His riches in glory? If you really trust Him, stop doubting Him. Just because the first bird caught a worm, it doesn't mean there are no more worms. It just means that yours is soon coming to the surface. And it will. So, trust in the promises of God. And have a providential day.

> *Behold the fowls of the air: for they sow not, neither do they reap, nor gather into barns; yet your heavenly Father feedeth them. Are ye not much better than they? Which of you by taking thought can add one cubit unto his stature? And why take ye thought for raiment? Consider the lilies of the field, how they grow; they toil not, neither do they spin: And yet I say unto you, That even Solomon in all his glory was not arrayed like one of these. (Matthew 6:26, 27, 28, 29)*

What are four things that you are grateful for? What would life be like without these things?

1. _____
2. _____
3. _____
4. _____

Today, give God a praise for the little things that you've always taken for granted.

No matter what you are going through, still praise God. Whether or not you praise Him, troubles will still come, stress will still exist, and you will still face obstacles. However, when you praise Him, those troubles seem as light afflictions. Stress is just another reason to trust Him. And obstacles are stepping stones to your victory. If you praise Him because of and in spite of, He will honor your praise. So, lift your voice in adoration to the King of Kings. And have a worshipful day.

In every thing give thanks: for this is the will of God in Christ Jesus concerning you. (1 Thessalonians 5:18)

Make today a praise day. Whatever you face, keep on praising.

Below, list all the reasons that you have for giving God praise.

Life has a way of teaching you the lesson you didn't want to learn. Each time you choose to do the thing you know you shouldn't, here comes life to stop you from making a bad choice and messing up. But you persist in having your own way, doing your own thing. Remember, being stubborn isn't a sign of maturity. It's a sign that you still have a long way to grow. If you're making bad choices just to show that you can make your own choices, you are your own person, or you can do what you want to, stop. It's better to follow the wisdom of a child than one's own arrogance. And it's more profitable to give in to reason than it is to admit later that you were wrong. Being stubborn doesn't win medals nor gain applause. But being humble and teachable will carry you for a lifetime. So just today, step back and let someone else take the lead, follow instead. And have a redirected day.

> *When] pride cometh, then cometh shame: but with the lowly [is] wisdom. (Proverbs 11:2)*
>
> *Pride [goeth] before destruction, and an haughty spirit before a fall. (Proverbs 16:18)*
>
> *And he said: "Truly I tell you, unless you change and become like little children, you will never enter the kingdom of heaven. (Matthew 18:3) (NIV)*

Self-Check:

Ask yourself the following questions and answer honestly. Then, think of how you can address each issue that requires change.

1. Do I always need to be right?
   _____

2. Am I willing to let others be in the limelight?
   _____

3. Do I feel like a failure when I am not recognized for what I have done?
   _____

4. Do others see me as a leader or a manager?
   _____

5. Am I teachable?
   _____

If you have people who say they love you completely, but they know nothing about your past, rethink the relationship. If they don't know why you cry at that movie or refuse to watch it, rethink that relationship. If they can't explain your fear of storms, insects, or yelling, rethink that relationship. Before Jesus forgave sin and filled those who were empty, He dealt with the individual's past. He knew about the five illicit husbands, the life of adultery, the tainted past of the woman with the alabaster box. He loved them enough to know what needed addressing. So, if you are loving a person for who they are now, you better know what made them who they are. And if someone is saying they don't need to know about your past, they aren't ready to love all of you. You may need to rethink your relationship and its importance, and be in it one hundred percent, or not at all. If you love as Christ, you must love one hundred. So, love completely. And have a knowledgeable day.

> *Before I formed you in the womb I knew you, before you were born I set you apart; I appointed you as a prophet to the nations. (Jeremiah 1:5)*
>
> *But God commendeth his love toward us, in that, while we were yet sinners, Christ died for us. (Romans 5:8)*
>
> *Wherefore receive ye one another, as Christ also received us to the glory of God. (Romans 15:7)*
>
> *Beloved, let us love one another: for love is of God; and every one that loveth is born of God, and knoweth God. He that loveth not knoweth not God; for God is love. (1 John 4:7, 8)*

What do you know about the past lives of those who are close to you? (Spouse, best friend, colleague)

_____
_____
_____
_____
_____
_____

What have you not wanted to know? Why?
_____
_____
_____
_____
_____

Make a determined effort to find out something new about those who you say are close to you. Don't be listening to judge. Listen to understand. See if there is something that can give you a better understanding of each person.

How many of you have dared to choose? You are all given options, but how many of you have "boldly dared" to choose? For instance, did you choose to love, in spite of the hate? Did you choose to laugh, in spite of the pain? Did you choose to forgive, in spite of the hurt? Did you choose to go on, in spite of the obstacles? Did you choose to believe, in spite of the doubts? Did you choose to live, in spite of the fear? Life is about choosing, and choosing to live. For your salvation, a choice was made. For your redemption, a choice was made. For your life, a choice was made. And it was the best choice possible. So, when it comes time for you to consider your options, make the best choice. Choose love, laughter, forgiveness, progress, faith, and life. Choose to live the best that God has offered for you and to you. And have a life changing day.

> *I call heaven and earth to record this day against you, that I have set before you life and death, blessing and cursing: therefore choose life, that both thou and thy seed may live: (Deuteronomy 30:19)*
>
> *Rejoicing in hope; patient in tribulation; continuing instant in prayer; (Romans 12:12)*

What are the options with which you are faced today?

1. _____
2. _____
3. _____
4. _____
5. _____

What choices will you make which you will be comfortable with?

_____
_____
_____
_____
_____

Remember, not choosing is a choice. Choose wisely.

Although life is all about changes, you don't have to change if you don't want to. You may be happy with yourself just the way you are. You may decide that you'd rather be perfect alone than imperfect among others. You may prefer to stand out and apart from the masses than become a functioning link in someone's chain. You never have to change if you'd rather be the center of attention. But if you'd rather let someone else shine for a while, you may need to change. The scripture states that you must consider others to be higher than you are. That takes change. That requires you to become less while others increase. While it may be a difficult task, it's not impossible. Remember, everyone in Christ becomes a new creation. That's change. And when you are changed internally, it's easy to see yourself in others and realize that someone else needs a push, a hand, a moment in the spotlight, so that they may change. So lift someone up today. And help them have a transforming day.

> *Let nothing be done through strife or vainglory; but in lowliness of mind let each esteem other better than themselves. (Philippians 2:3)*

What are some changes that you see are needed around you, on the job, in your home, in your relationships?

_____
_____
_____
_____

How can you change to affect these changes?

_____
_____
_____
_____

Your life is someone's guidebook. Be the change that you want to see in the world, and others will change as well.

What would you do if tomorrow you woke up and all of your family members were gone? All your friends were gone? All your acquaintances were gone? What if all of your neighbors were gone? What would you do? Would you wonder where they were? Would you hazard a guess as to where they were? Or would you know for a fact where they were? Would you wonder if something bad had occurred? Would you think that they had all deserted you? Would you know if they had all been raptured? How would you feel knowing that you were left behind? What if that were today? If you're thinking right now, "what if," then you need to make sure today. What if there was no tomorrow? Tomorrow is never a guarantee. But today is. He said, today, if you will hear my voice, harden not your heart. And remember, today is not a guarantee either. So while you have a chance to live, live it well. But when you have a chance to live eternally, don't let it pass you by. Harken to His call. And have a redeemed day.

> *And then shall appear the sign of the Son of man in heaven: and then shall all the tribes of the earth mourn, and they shall see the Son of man coming in the clouds of heaven with power and great glory. And he shall send his angels with a great sound of a trumpet, and they shall gather together his elect from the four winds, from one end of heaven to the other. (Matthew 24:30, 31)*

> *For the Lord himself shall descend from heaven with a shout, with the voice of the archangel, and with the trump of God: and the dead in Christ shall rise first: Then we which are alive and remain shall be caught up together with them in the clouds, to meet the Lord in the air: and so shall we ever be with the Lord. Wherefore comfort one another with these words. (1 Thessalonians 4:16, 17, 18)*

> *While it is said, To day if ye will hear his voice, harden not your hearts, as in the provocation. (Hebrews 3:15)*

What do you need to do today to be sure that if the Lord returned today, you would be ready?

_____

_____

_____

_____

You've heard it said that people come into your life for a reason or a season. But what if you're not aware of the reason or the season? What if you misread the cues and think they are there for your good when they aren't? What if you think they're there to love you when they're ready to leave you? And how do you know when the season is over? How do you know that it's time to let go when you just want to hold on? How do you know that today is the end of the journey, when you were planning for more tomorrows? You may never know before the time, but you should know that there is a time for everything under heaven. There's a time to laugh and a time to cry; a time to love and a time to hate. Everything has a season. So, don't be dismayed. Just trust that God is in control of your season. He determines the rainstorm and the sunshine, and he controls every wind that will blow your way. So, trust Him that a new season is coming your way. And have a refreshing day.

> *To every thing there is a season, and a time to every purpose under the heaven: A time to weep, and a time to laugh; a time to mourn, and a time to dance; A time to love, and a time to hate; a time of war, and a time of peace. (Ecclesiastes 3:1, 4, 8)*

Consider the persons who have come into your life.

Determine who is there just for a reason or a season.

What is the purpose of each person?

_____

_____

_____

_____

Would you know when their time was up in your life?

_____

Are you prepared to let them go when they have fulfilled their purpose?

_____

Be prepare for doors to close, but be ready for God to open new doors for you.

Remember, it's ok to look back sometimes. But don't get caught up in what's behind and miss what is ahead. The more time you spend looking behind you, the less time you have to spend on moving forward. And while you're busy with the things of the past, there is someone who is waiting to pass you by in this game of life. While there's nothing wrong with, sometimes, being passed on the side of the road, if you're stuck in the mire of past guilt, past shame, or past self-condemnation, you will never be able to push the gears hard enough to get yourself unstuck. So, while you may stop for a minute to reminisce, don't forget to keep the focus on what is before you. Better yet, forget the things that are behind, those things which can so easily beset you. Let the things of Christ and the mind of Christ be your motivation. And have a progressive day.

> *Brethren, I count not myself to have apprehended: but this one thing I do, forgetting those things which are behind, and reaching forth unto those things which are before, I press toward the mark for the prize of the high calling of God in Christ Jesus. (Philippians 3:13-14)*

What is the past guilt, or shame, or condemnation that has you grounded in your progress?

_____

_____

_____

_____

What steps can you take to eliminate that guilt, remove that shame, and lift that condemnation?

_____

_____

_____

_____

Remember, your past is just an opportunity for God to show you how great his cleansing power is. Just as He forgives without condemnation, so must you live without condemnation.

What is your definition of beauty? Is beauty the face that you see in the mirror? Is beauty the color of someone's skin, her hair, the shape of her body, the way she walks? Or is beauty the sound of his voice, his laughter, his commanding presence? What is beauty? If beauty is the outward reflection or appearance of what's inside, then beauty should be the heart that cares, that shares, that understands. Beauty should be the hand reaching down to lift up one who stumbles and falls, the nights spent in prayer, the tears that are shed, the unconditional love radiating from a giving heart. But without the inward love of God, there can be no manifestation of beauty. Beauty says, "I love you in spite of." That is true beauty. Do not let what you are looking for, or at, be the outward show of beauty, for that will fail. Seek the inward beauty of Christ that will never fade away. And have a spiritually beautified day.

> *Whose adorning let it not be that outward adorning of plaiting the hair, and of wearing of gold, or of putting on of apparel; But let it be the hidden man of the heart, in that which is not corruptible, even the ornament of a meek and quiet spirit, which is in the sight of God of great price. (1 Peter 3:3, 4)*

What is your definition of beauty?

_____
_____
_____
_____

Would others consider you to be a beautiful person, with the beauty on the outside, reflecting what is on the inside?

_____
_____
_____
_____

If you find any inner beauty flaw, allow the love to God to fill you with His beauty and grace. He will beautify the meek with His salvation.

When it's time to leave on a journey, whether there is rain or sun, snow or sleet, you still pack your bags in preparation. You might call ahead, but not to cancel. You call to verify that the flight is still scheduled. You hope and pray that the plane will leave, because you've already paid the price. Then, if the airline cancels the flight, you accept the change. You rearrange your schedule to fit their schedule. You lose a day, or several hours, but you don't ever leave the airline for another. You've already paid the price. But haven't you already paid the price in your relationships and in your friendships. So why is it easy for you to walk away, throw away all that you've worked for, or try another relationship? Despite all the setbacks, the rescheduling, and the losses, Christ didn't give up on you. So, don't give up on what you've paid so dear a price for. Remember, the reward goes to those who faint not, and who stay the course. So, stay. And have a rewarding day.

> *And let us not be weary in well doing: for in due season we shall reap, if we faint not. (Galatians 6:9)*

What are some reasons that you have for wanting to walk away from your relationships?

1. _____
2. _____
3. _____
4. _____

What have you tried in order to resolve your issues?

1. _____
2. _____
3. _____
4. _____

Have you tried prayer? Remember, prayer changes both things and persons. Don't give up until there is nothing left to hold on to.

Are you superstitious? Do you believe that if you break a mirror or walk under a ladder, it's seven years bad luck? Do you avoid walking on cracks on the sidewalk because of what others say it will do to your mother? What about that black cat walking across your path? Do you still fear him? Do you still turn around at the front door and enter backwards, just so those spirits won't follow behind you? You still believe in these things, but you can't believe that Jesus is the Son of God? Do you struggle with the fact that He died and rose again? You can't conceive of the idea that with faith in Him, all things are possible, but you believe that trusting in a rabbit's tail, or a horse's shoe, will protect you? Its time you faced the truth. No supernatural power can harm you if you have Jesus. And none can save or protect you unless it comes from Jesus. All it takes is simple faith in the blood of Jesus. So, trade your superstitions for faith. And have a deliverance day.

> *Neither is there salvation in any other: for there is none other name under heaven given among men, whereby we must be saved. (Acts 4:12)*

What is your superstition?

_____
_____
_____

Have you proven that it works? How?

_____
_____
_____

Have you proven that faith in Jesus works? How?

_____
_____
_____

Today, stop fearing the unknown and start trusting the God who controls the unknown. If faith in God works, then faith is greater than all your fears.

Does praying seem to be the latest fad? You get sick, you pray. Bills to pay, you pray. Job looking insecure, you pray. Relationship not working so well, you pray. People talking about you, you pray. Yet with all the praying, you aren't getting delivered? So, what are you really telling God when you pray? It is His will that: every need be supplied, every burden be lifted, you be prosperous and in good health, you be the lender and not the borrower, the head and not the tail. So instead of telling God what He can do, tell your problems what God can do. Stop seeing your problems as if they are problems for God. It's only a problem if He can't handle it, and nothing is too hard for God to do. Speak to your problem as if it was already solved, your burden as if it was already lifted, and your situation as if it was already fixed. Then instead of praying for deliverance, praise God for the deliverance. Thank Him for what has already been done. And have a celebratory day.

> *Therefore I say unto you, Take no thought for your life, what ye shall eat, or what ye shall drink; nor yet for your body, what ye shall put on. Is not the life more than meat, and the body than raiment? Behold the fowls of the air: for they sow not, neither do they reap, nor gather into barns; yet your heavenly Father feedeth them. Are ye not much better than they? Which of you by taking thought can add one cubit unto his stature? And why take ye thought for raiment? Consider the lilies of the field, how they grow; they toil not, neither do they spin: And yet I say unto you, That even Solomon in all his glory was not arrayed like one of these. Wherefore, if God so clothe the grass of the field, which to day is, and to morrow is cast into the oven, shall he not much more clothe you, O ye of little faith? Therefore take no thought, saying, What shall we eat? or, What shall we drink? or, Wherewithal shall we be clothed? (For after all these things do the Gentiles seek:) for your heavenly Father knoweth that ye have need of all these things. But seek ye first the kingdom of God, and his righteousness; and all these things shall be added unto you. (Matthew 6:25—33)*

How do you pray when you pray? Be honest. Write your usual prayer. Is it worded according to the will of God?
_____
_____
_____
_____

Today, instead of reminding God about the things that are wrong, start praising Him for the things that are right. Remember that your big problems are small situations for God to handle.

Then start declaring that you are victorious, you are delivered, your chains have been broken, etc. Remember, God operates on your praise. He lives in your praise, and He responds to your praise.

If you are sitting there reliving your "PAST", regretting your PAST, or just hating yourself because of your PAST, it's time to stop. Don't you know what your PAST is? Your P.A.S.T. is "Patience And Strength Tested." While you were in your mess, going through your mess, or getting out of your mess, your patience was being tested. You were being assessed and evaluated. You were being checked for endurance and faith. And while you were being challenged, beat down, and intentionally overlooked, your strength was being tested. You were being prepared for your future spiritual battles, the divine call, and the appointment that would be placed on your life. So, don't let your test be for nothing. Show the enemy that your P.A.S.T is merely the means to your master's degree in victory. And the next time you come face to face with history, tell it you already passed that test, and you're moving to a higher level. So, leave the past in the past. And have a forward-looking day.

> *Remember ye not the former things, neither consider the things of old. Behold, I will do a new thing; now it shall spring forth; shall ye not know it? I will even make a way in the wilderness, and rivers in the desert. (Isaiah 43:18, 19)*
>
> *Knowing this, that the trying of your faith worketh patience. But let patience have her perfect work, that ye may be perfect and entire, wanting nothing. (James 1:3, 4)*
>
> *Wherein ye greatly rejoice, though now for a season, if need be, ye are in heaviness through manifold temptations: That the trial of your faith, being much more precious than of gold that perisheth, though it be tried with fire, might be found unto praise and honour and glory at the appearing of Jesus Christ: (1 Peter 1:6, 7)*

What has been your greatest test from your past, so far?

_____

_____

_____

How has it tested your patience and strength?

_____

_____

_____

Tell yourself, "I'm still standing."

Now write a list of as many victories as possible which you have overcome already this year. You'll see that you passed your test, over and over.

What does it mean to have the angels of the Lord with you? Does it mean that no weapon will be formed against you? Does it mean that no tongue will rise up in judgment? Does it mean that you will not dash your foot against a stone? The scripture never said that weapons wouldn't form. And it doesn't say that others won't condemn or judge you. Neither does it say that you won't stumble or fall. But it does promise that His angels will have charge over you. They will bear you in their hands. They will encamp round about you. They will deliver you. The enemy will attack you, hinder your progress, despise you, talk about you, ensnare and tempt you. But fear not. God had dispatched His ministering angel to sustain you. Just trust that the hand being offered is of the Lord, for He will send His angels to restore you. They are His messengers to you. Allow them to fulfill His promise of mercy in your life. And have a divinely favored day.

> *For he shall give his angels charge over thee, to keep thee in all thy ways. They shall bear thee up in their hands, lest thou dash thy foot against a stone. ... He shall call upon me, and I will answer him: I will be with him in trouble; I will deliver him, and honour him. (Psalms 91:11, 12, 15)*

> *No weapon that is formed against thee shall prosper; and every tongue that shall rise against thee in judgment thou shalt condemn. This is the heritage of the servants of the Lord, and their righteousness is of me, saith the Lord. (Isaiah 54:17)*

What do you need protection from, or in, today?

_____

_____

_____

_____

Take the suggested scriptures above with you and place them where the enemy can see them. Write them on your heart. Release them into the atmosphere, and the angels will be commanded to stand guard over you. Today, use the weapon of spiritual warfare against your enemies.

Ever wonder why your past, current, and future situations are the same? It's because you've been sitting on the same rock, watching the same grass, pruning the same bush, and reaping the same fruit. Yet you expect something different to occur? You've heard that for something different to occur, you have to try something different. So, move the rock you're sitting on and see what's buried beneath. There're things you've been sitting on which need to be turned over and reassessed. The grass you've been watching is only greener because you're sitting in the shade on that rock. If you leave your comfort zone, you'll find that you don't need greener grass at all. You just need to take off the smeared glasses so that you can see what's in front of you. The bush you've been pruning isn't even yours. Stop lighting someone else's fire while yours is dying. And the fruit you've been reaping will be different and better when you tend your own garden. So, get moving. And have a productive day.

> *And that ye study to be quiet, and to do your own business, and to work with your own hands, as we commanded you; That ye may walk honestly toward them that are without, and that ye may have lack of nothing. (1 Thessalonians 4:11, 12)*

Whose garden are you tending, instead of your own?
_____
_____
_____

What seed have you sown to reap the harvest you are awaiting?
_____
_____
_____

How long are you willing to wait to see if the crop will be "good enough"?
_____
_____
_____

To get different, you need to attempt different. So, make today a day of movement. Do something different.
___
___
___

(At the end of your day, respond to the question below.)

What did you do different today, and what was the outcome?
___
___

When your life begins to feel like a wrong-train ride, it's time to consider your options. You can stand at the door and watch the stations go by, you can go for the ride and just enjoy the views, or you can sadly wish you were at the station you just passed by. But seeing life flash by, watching the views, or wishing that you were where you aren't in life, doesn't get you off the train and on to better things. So, you could choose option four. Learn the route and plan how to never make the mistake of getting on the wrong train again. When you realize that you've made a mistake: you slipped up, went the wrong direction, or made the wrong decisions in your life, learn from your mistakes. And remember, there's always a conductor that you can ask for directions, just as you can seek God's direction in all your decisions. So, don't stay on the wrong train and end up hopelessly lost. You have choice. Choose to reroute your plan and purpose, with God's leading. And have a redirected day

> *And if it seem evil unto you to serve the Lord, choose you this day whom ye will serve; whether the gods which your fathers served that were on the other side of the flood, or the gods of the Amorites, in whose land ye dwell: but as for me and my house, we will serve the Lord. (Joshua 24:15)*

> *Therefore thus saith the Lord, If thou return, then will I bring thee again, and thou shalt stand before me: and if thou take forth the precious from the vile, thou shalt be as my mouth: let them return unto thee; but return not thou unto them. (Jeremiah 15:19)*

What is one mistake which you made in the past six months that you have learned a lesson from? What is the lesson learned?

_____

_____

_____

What is your plan for the next time you are in a similar situation?

_____

_____

_____

Be sure to keep that plan at the forefront of your memory the next time you are going into the battle.

Throughout your life of growth, there are lessons that you have to learn. You have to learn your letters, numbers, and correct grammar. You need to learn how to act in any given situation. And you come to learn who to trust and who to avoid. But in all of these lessons, you are never taught how to depend on Jesus. And if there's one thing that you need to learn, it's how to lean on Jesus. But this lesson can only be learned from experience. You have to stumble to learn that He will catch you. You have to fall down to learn that He will pick you up. You have to be in the struggle to learn that He will fight your battle. You have to be at the end of your hope to learn that He will make a way. No schoolroom lesson that you are taught guarantees that you will learn anything. But if you trust God, you will never forget how great His mercy can be. So, let your life be your schoolroom. Learn what it means to depend on Jesus. And have an enlightened day.

> *And they that know thy name will put their trust in thee: for thou, Lord, hast not forsaken them that seek thee. (Psalm 9:10)*

> *Trust in the Lord with all thine heart; and lean not unto thine own understanding. In all thy ways acknowledge him, and he shall direct thy paths. (Proverbs 3:5, 6)*

> *And, behold, there arose a great tempest in the sea, insomuch that the ship was covered with the waves: but he was asleep. And his disciples came to him, and awoke him, saying, Lord, save us: we perish. And he saith unto them, Why are ye fearful, O ye of little faith? Then he arose, and rebuked the winds and the sea; and there was a great calm. (Matthew 8:24, 25, 26)*

Over the course of your Christian walk, what have you learned about depending on Jesus?

_____
_____
_____
_____
_____

What have you learned over the past six months?
_____
_____
_____
_____

What have you learned over the past week?
_____
_____
_____
_____

Now give Him a genuine praise.

How many of you in the heat of an argument have been accused of, or have accused someone of, acting like a child? Was the person being loving and trusting? Was he showing his dependency on you? Was she allowing you to be the adult, allowing you to control and lead the way? Or was he pouting and throwing a tantrum? Was she loud and offensive and trying to take the reins out of your hands? If it was the latter, then that wasn't acting like a child. That behavior is not allowed in the kingdom of God. There is no pouting, yelling, or defying in the kingdom of God. So, the next time you want to be as a little child, you have to be gentle, loving, and aware of your reliance on the savior. And when you feel the need to take control, remember that God is in control. When you allow Him to hold the reins, you won't have to be concerned about others trying to take it from you. So humble yourself under the divine authority of Christ. And have a divinely reliant day.

> *And said, Verily I say unto you, Except ye be converted, and become as little children, ye shall not enter into the kingdom of heaven. (Matthew 18:3)*
>
> *But Jesus said, Suffer little children, and forbid them not, to come unto me: for of such is the kingdom of heaven. (Matthew 19:14)*
>
> *Humble yourselves in the sight of the Lord, and he shall lift you up. Speak not evil one of another, brethren. He that speaketh evil of his brother, and judgeth his brother, speaketh evil of the law, and judgeth the law: but if thou judge the law, thou art not a doer of the law, but a judge. (James 4:10, 11)*
>
> *Behold, what manner of love the Father hath bestowed upon us, that we should be called the sons of God: therefore the world knoweth us not, because it knew him not. (1 John 3:1)*

What does it mean to you to be child-like?

_____

_____

_____

_____

If the kingdom of God belongs to those who are as little children, would your attitude allow you access? Why or why not?
_____
_____
_____
_____

Today, have a conversation with God, approaching Him in a child-like manner. Let Him be in control. Listen to what He is saying to you. Be aware of this attitude the next time you find yourself in an argument or disagreement.

Have you ever had someone who knew you so well, that before you finished asking a question, they were providing an answer? Or someone whom if you paused in the middle of your sentence, they finished it for you? What if you wanted something to eat or drink, is there someone who just knows what you need, and when you need it? It is like that when you are connected to God. He knows what you are about to say before you say it, and what you need before you ask. He has already provided all that you desire. That's why He says that if you ask anything in His name, believing, it shall be done. So, ask with the assurance that He knows your needs, desires, hopes, and dreams. And He's willing to supply. You just have to tell Him. For although He knows what you desire, He still wants to hear your voice. So, seek Him while He may be found, and call upon Him while He is near. And have a bountiful day.

> *But when ye pray, use not vain repetitions, as the heathen do: for they think that they shall be heard for their much speaking. Be not ye therefore like unto them: for your Father knoweth what things ye have need of, before ye ask him. (Matthew 6:7, 8)*

> *And whatsoever ye shall ask in my name, that will I do, that the Father may be glorified in the Son. If ye shall ask any thing in my name, I will do it. (John 14:13, 14)*

What do you desire from God today?

_____
_____
_____
_____

Just tell Him, and open yourself to receive.

There has to be a reason why you get up every morning and choose to be. You may choose to be happy, to be content, to laugh, or to love. Or you may choose to be unhappy, to be dissatisfied, to cry, or to hate. Whatever, the options, you must choose. So, before you choose, think of the souls you will encounter throughout your day. Will you be a builder or a destroyer? Will you be a helper or a hinderer? Will you be the one to point the way or will you be the stumbling block? Remember, you will be called to give an account of what you have done, whether it be good or whether it be evil. So intentionally choose to bless someone with a smile, a hug, or a cheerful word as you travel along, so that your day be a day of purpose. Simply choose to love. And have an influential day.

> *So then every one of us shall give account of himself to God. (Romans 14:12)*

> *For we must all appear before the judgment seat of Christ; that every one may receive the things done in his body, according to that he hath done, whether it be good or bad. (2 Corinthians 5:10)*

What intentional choices will you make today?

_____

_____

_____

_____

How will you impact:

1. A Child
2. A family member
3. A friend
4. A colleague
5. A stranger

The choice is up to you.

The realization that you are wonderfully created in the image of God should make you daily one of two things. You should be so excited that you want to tell about it. You want everyone to know that you are special, and they are too. You want them to be amazed with you at the thought that the creator of heaven and earth created you. When you think of the work of His hand, the thought that went into your being, the awesome wisdom, knowledge, and understanding that produced your living soul, you should just want to shout. On the other hand, when you realize that you were an intentional creation, you should be humbled. That God, the Omnipotent, the Omniscient, the Omnipresent One, would think enough of you, to know you before you were formed in your mother's womb, to determine your existence; you should bow in humble praise and worship. Let Him know with a grateful and penitent heart that He is all you need. He is. So, honor Him with your living. And have a humble day.

> *So God created man in his own image, in the image of God created he him; male and female created he them. (Genesis 1:27)*
>
> *I will praise thee; for I am fearfully and wonderfully made: marvellous are thy works; and that my soul knoweth right well. (Psalm 139:14)*
>
> *Before I formed thee in the belly I knew thee; and before thou camest forth out of the womb I sanctified thee, and I ordained thee a prophet unto the nations. (Jeremiah 1:5)*

What is there about the love of God towards you which humbles you?

_____
_____
_____
_____

Let Him know how much you appreciate Him. He is waiting to hear from you.

_____
_____
_____
_____

If your faith has been tested, did you pass the test? It's one thing to say that you live by faith, but another to show that you are living faith. You can claim that you can do all things through Christ, but if nothing in being done, then, where is your faith? You can stand and declare that nothing is impossible with God, but if you are still facing impossible obstacles, then you are failing every test. Faith without works is dead. If there are no results to your faith talk, there is no reality to your faith walk. Remember, without faith, it is impossible to please God. So, if you are going to claim that you are walking by faith, make sure that you are walking in victory, and coming out of every situation. Live by faith. Walk your talk. And have an evidence and substance-based day.

> *But without faith it is impossible to please him: for he that cometh to God must believe that he is, and that he is a rewarder of them that diligently seek him. (Hebrews 11:6)*
>
> *What doth it profit, my brethren, though a man say he hath faith, and have not works? can faith save him? Even so faith, if it hath not works, is dead, being alone. Yea, a man may say, Thou hast faith, and I have works: shew me thy faith without thy works, and I will shew thee my faith by my works. For as the body without the spirit is dead, so faith without works is dead also. (James 2:14, 17, 18, 26)*

What is your faith testimony that you will share this week?

_____
_____
_____
_____
_____
_____
_____

What does it mean to wait? Does it mean to put off or delay? Or does it mean to anticipate, expect, or hope? Why do you wait? Why do you put your life, your dreams, your desires on hold, waiting? And will you be rewarded, or disappointed? Is waiting merely a form of procrastination? When you say you will wait until your change comes, what are you expecting to change? Will you even know when it happens? Many of you are waiting, and waiting hopelessly. You know "that" change isn't coming, but you wait. You hold on, hopelessly. It's time to stop waiting hopelessly, and start waiting patiently. Start preparing for your change. Start anticipating your day of release, redemption, and restoration. In Christ there is hope. When you wait on Him, it is with the knowledge that something will happen, and things will get better. You'll even know when things have changed. So set your hopes on a God who never fails. Just wait on Him and be of good courage. And have a hope-full day.

> Wait on the Lord: be of good courage, and he shall strengthen thine heart: wait, I say, on the Lord. (Psalm 27:14)
>
> I waited patiently for the Lord; and he inclined unto me, and heard my cry. He brought me up also out of an horrible pit, out of the miry clay, and set my feet upon a rock, and established my goings. And he hath put a new song in my mouth, even praise unto our God: many shall see it, and fear, and shall trust in the Lord. (Psalm 40:1, 2, 3)
>
> But they that wait upon the Lord shall renew their strength; they shall mount up with wings as eagles; they shall run, and not be weary; and they shall walk, and not faint. (Isaiah 40:31)

If God should send your miracle today, would you be ready to receive it? What do you still need to do to be ready?

_____

_____

_____

_____

Don't let it pass you by. Be ready to receive, even as you wait to receive.

_____

_____

If you have reached a dark place in your life, hold on. Not every dark place is a bad place. Sometimes you need to get out of the light in order to find yourself. And sometimes you need to be in the shade in order to appreciate the light. And often, in the dark place, you begin to really see who's there for you. The psalmist said even though he walked through the valley of the shadow of death, he would not fear, because God was with him. So, sometimes, you have to go through the darkest situation to feel the presence of God with you. While it might not be comfortable in the darkness, and while it might take all your faith to stay in the dark until you find yourself, the darkness serves a purpose. When you finally come out of the darkness, you'll be able to help someone else through their dark time. In short, there's a reason for the dark. So just trust the light of God to get you through. And have a purpose-full day

> *Yea, though I walk through the valley of the shadow of death, I will fear no evil: for thou art with me; thy rod and thy staff they comfort me. (Psalm 23:4)*
>
> *Yea, the darkness hideth not from thee; but the night shineth as the day: the darkness and the light are both alike to thee. (Psalm 139:12)*
>
> *And I will bring the blind by a way that they knew not; I will lead them in paths that they have not known: I will make darkness light before them, and crooked things straight. These things will I do unto them, and not forsake them. (Isaiah 42:16)*

In the midst of your dark storm, allow yourself to be drawn closer to the light of Christ. Spend time in finding who you are, what you really desire, and what God has purposed for your life.

Use the dark moments to allow God to reveal Himself to you. Don't rush the process.

When you come out of the darkness, use your experience to help someone out of their darkness.

Tell your story for others to find the light.

_____

_____

_____

If you forgot everything and everyone you know, would you still exist? If the past no longer existed, would you still be who you are? If you had no responsibilities or cares, would you still find something to worry about? If tomorrow never came, would today matter more? Life is not about the stress and worries that you can accumulate. It's about the moment, where you are right now. It's about the person standing in front of you at this moment. It's about the attitude that you face today with. The scripture says, "Take no thought for tomorrow." For enough are the cares that tomorrow has. There are sufficient things waiting for you to think about tomorrow. There is enough evil that awaits you, tomorrow. But today needs your attention. Your spouse needs your attention, today. Your children need your attention, today. You need your attention, today. So why clutter today with tomorrow's problems? Just trust in the God who holds tomorrow. And have a stress-free day.

> *Take therefore no thought for the morrow: for the morrow shall take thought for the things of itself. Sufficient unto the day is the evil thereof. (Matthew 6:34)*

Who needs your attention today? Put everything aside and spend the day with that special someone, a son or daughter, an elderly parent. Someone needs your attention.

Discuss the highlights of your day here.

_____
_____
_____
_____
_____

Note the many time during your day that you didn't worry about tomorrow. That's what living today is all about.

_____
_____
_____

If war was declared tomorrow, would you go to fight? Would you be prepared to face the enemy? Would you be able to hold your ground in spite of all the darts that would be sent at you? Would you be willing to follow the leadership of the one in charge? Or would you hide, pretend you didn't get the call, or act like it's not your fight? Would you try things your own way, or would you in the heat of the battle, throw up your hands and declare that you surrender? Note that if you are a child of God, the war has already been declared. You are already facing the darts and the sword of the enemy. But be confident that this battle is in the hand of the Captain of the Host, and He never runs from a challenge. So, suit up in the armor of righteousness, stand fast, hold your post, quit ye like soldiers of the heavenly King. And have a battle-ready day.

> *Watch ye, stand fast in the faith, quit you like men, be strong. (1 Corinthians 16:13)*

> *Put on the whole armour of God, that ye may be able to stand against the wiles of the devil... Wherefore take unto you the whole armour of God, that ye may be able to withstand in the evil day, and having done all, to stand. Stand therefore, having your loins girt about with truth, and having on the breastplate of righteousness (Ephesians 6:11, 13, 14)*

Write a declaration today to stay in the fight, no matter the cost.

_____
_____
_____
_____
_____
_____
_____

After you have made your declaration, return to the opening message of the book and see if you have truly been transformed over the past six months. If you can truly declare that you have let go of all that was hindering your growth when you started on this journey, then you are in the battle to stay; then you have successfully completed your journey.

Thank you for taking that journey with me.